Perth
The Fair City

Perth
The Fair City

DAVID GRAHAM-CAMPBELL

JOHN DONALD PUBLISHERS LTD
EDINBURGH

The colour illustrations on the
front cover are reproduced by courtesy
of Perthshire Tourist Board, and the sketch of
St John's Kirk by courtesy of the friends
of St John's Kirk, Perth.

ISBN 0 85976 382 X

British Library Cataloguing in Publication Data
A catalogue record for this book is available from the British Library.

Typeset by ROM-Data Corporation Ltd, Falmouth, Cornwall.
Printed in Great Britain by Bell & Bain Ltd, Glasgow.

Acknowledgements

I should like to express my thanks to those who have read various chapters in draft, for their suggestions and corrections, and most of all to the late Dr Margaret Stewart, to whom Perth owes so much for her strenuous efforts to draw attention to Perth's heritage 'before it is too late', for her own writings and for the part she played in the formation of the Perth Civic Trust. I am indebted to the authors of a number of publications listed below, most of which are available from the sales centre in the Sandeman Library and in some branch libraries.

Bogden, N.Q., and Wordsworth, J.W., *The Mediaeval Excavations at the High Street, Perth 1975-6*, the original drawings by Mr Sandy Yule
Cameron, Kenneth J., *The Schoolmaster Engineer* [Adam Anderson]
Fothergill, R. *A History of King James VI Hospital*
Fothergill, R. *Kinnoull, Bridgend and Barnhill*
Fothergill, R. *What's in a Name?*
Friends of St John's Kirk, *Illustrated Notes on the Stained Glass Windows and the Mediaeval Silver*
Holdsworth, Philip, Perth. *The Archaeology of the Mediaeval Town*.
Perth Town Council. *Walks in Perth*
Perth Civic Trust. *Perth. A Town Survey*
Robson, Eric, *Branklyn*
Scottish Urban Archaeological Trust. *Greyfriars*
Simpson, W. Douglas, *A History of St John's Kirk, Perth*
Stavert, Marion L, *Perth. A Short History*
Stewart, M.E.C. and Thomas, L.M. *It will soon be too late*

I am also grateful to the authors of the following books:

Bannerman, G. *Saints Alive*
Harvey, A.G., *Douglas of the Forests*
House, J. *Pride of Perth*
Marshall, W., *Historic Scenes in Perthshire*
Willsher, Betty and Doreen Hunter. *Stones. 18th Century Scottish Gravestones*

The Statistical Account of Scotland, 1793
The New Statistical Account of Scotland, 1845
The Third Statistical Account of Scotland, 1964.

I must express special thanks to Mr F.J. Guthrie, the District Librarian, and to the staff of the Sandeman Library, who have been ever helpful, and my thanks are due to the following for permission to quote from their writings: Professor A. Duncan, Mr Philip Holdsworth, Mr N.A. Bogdon, Miss R. Fothergill, Mr J.A. McCowan, Mr G. Bannerman.

The Curators of the Signet Library and of the Perth Archives have kindly allowed me to quote from material in their possession.

The passage from the Journal of David Douglas is copyright of the Trustees of the Royal Botanic Gardens, Kew, and is reproduced with their permission.

Not least, I am indebted to the Rev. Fergus Harris for correcting the proofs, and to my son, James Graham-Campbell for his encouragement and assistance with the illustrations.

Contents

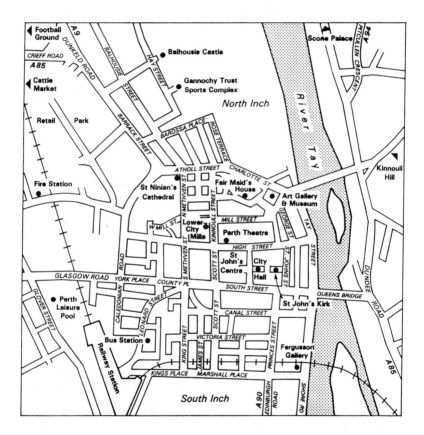

Location Map

CHAPTER ONE

The Fair City

For over two hundred years now, Perth has claimed to be 'The Fair City' but recently (after a serious academic study) it has independently been declared to be the fairest city of all in the United Kingdom, that is, amongst the middle-sized cities administered by District Councils. A group from Strathclyde and Glasgow Universities, interested in the 'quality of life' wanted to find out what mattered most to people when they were choosing a city to live in. They considered a large number of factors from which they selected some forty-six as being the most likely to influence people, such things as: The job market; the housing market; the cost of living and its relation to local wages; the environment and pollution; access to areas of scenic beauty; recreational facilities; good local health care; education; climate; shopping facilities, and so on. After studying 145 district council areas, they awarded the first prize to Perth. Not, in fact, a very surprising decision to those who live there. Indeed, nine hundred years ago, people were already voting with their feet, though sometimes for rather different reasons than those which prevail today, if only because few people in the Middle Ages had much choice as to where they could live. Only kings and their courtiers, monks and friars and a handful of successful merchants had such a choice.

In earliest times, ease of communications probably mattered most, and Perth was accessible up the Tay. Then the Romans found that Perth was their most suitable crossing place over the river as they made their way farther north, because here lay the first non-tidal ford. As tracks and then primitive roads came into existence, these tended to converge on Perth.

Another prime consideration in early days was safety, and this played a considerable part in Kenneth MacAlpine's

1

decision to set up the headquarters of his newly united Kingdom of the Picts and the Scots—not in his beautiful Argyll, but in Perthshire, where he was better defended against the harassing Norsemen as they drove up the sea lochs of the West coast. Religion affected the issue too. Already established at Scone was a community of Culdees, to which Alexander I soon added a well-endowed Augustinian abbey.

As Kings became more powerful—and richer—they wanted more in the way of luxuries and were less content with what the immediate locality could provide; more elaborate materials would have to be imported to make their robes. Here again Perth was suitable in that the tidal Tay enabled small boats to reach and unload their cargoes there, at a wharf near where the modern High Street reaches the river. This became the nucleus of the burgh, with the Watergate its first street alongside the river, followed by the High Street at right angles to it.

Trade would have been further augmented by the founding of other religious houses and by the granting of a charter by King David I, who also either built or enlarged the parish church and dedicated it to St John The Baptist; hence Perth's alternative name, St Johnstone. His grandson, Alexander II, endowed what was to be an important community of Dominicans (or Blackfriars) just to the north of the burgh where there was also a royal castle—probably little more than a mound of earth with a timber wall and a timber chapel. Later kings added a Carmelite (or Whitefriars) friary to the west of the town (Alexander III) and a Charterhouse near to the modern railway station (James I). And, if that were not enough, Laurence, 1st Lord Oliphant, built a Franciscan friary just to the east of the burgh walls. Two nunneries were dedicated to St Leonard and St Mary Magdalene.

The later monasteries may have been better endowed, but the sacred place of greatest significance remained that of Scone. Here was the stone on which the King would be placed, not in the chapel where it was kept for safety, but on a small mound outside. No crown was placed upon his head in early days; no bishop took the principal part; the privilege of placing the candidate on the stone was reserved for the lay subject who was felt to have the hereditary right. And then, when some sort of oath had been sworn that king and people would observe their obligations to each other, there came a recitation of a long list of kings going back well into the mists of tradition.

Returning to the needs of defence, Perth had other attractions. Rather unusually for a Scottish burgh, it was walled on the three sides which were not already protected by the river. And outside the walls a sort of moat had to be crossed before the main defences could be scaled or battered by an attacker. These walls have long since crumbled or been plundered when stone was wanted for building, but their exact line is still known, because the moat still exists although the lade itself is now mostly covered over. Short stretches may be seen by the Lower City Mills and at the rear of the Museum but the best view is obtained from a few yards along the road to Crieff.

The Town Lade as it emerges from the Lower City Mills.

In fact the town's 'moat' was not originally dug for defensive purposes* but to create a 'lade', a channel to provide a constant flow of water to turn the wheels of grain and other mills. Just who devised the scheme or who carried it out in those pick-and-shovel days is not known, but some very early benefactor organised the taking of water from the River Almond, some four miles to the north of the burgh (near Huntingtower Castle) to make a short cut to the north-western outskirts of Perth, where the grain mills were situated. Thence the stream was directed through various useful channels back to join the Tay. The easiest place nowadays to see the lade is from near where the Crieff road crosses the railway. Here steps lead down on either side of the road to the path beside the lade which can then be followed upstream through the town's outskirts or, for a shorter distance, downstream to the modern City Mills Hotel and the recently refurbished Lower City Mills, after which it passes below ground. A closer appreciation of its branches underground must wait for a later chapter where a walk is taken to demonstrate the exact boundaries of medieval Perth. However, since the town remained within these boundaries for nearly 700 years a look at the very accurate map drawn by Rutherford in 1774 will help. From the capital L (the granaries) at the top right-hand corner of the map, one branch flows almost straight down eastwards until it rejoins the river near the W (or 'Deadland'). This branch now flows beneath Mill Street. The other main branch turns sharp right just above the capital O (or 'Principal Cotton Manufactory') and proceeds past the heads of the High Street and South Street until it curves eastwards by the side of what was then called Spy Ridge—that is, it flows beneath the present-day Methven Street, Canal Crescent and Canal Street. That branch has to be taken on trust, being below ground, but the former can be seen in comfort, flowing and turning a wheel beneath a heavy glass panel let into the floor

*It is however possible that the lades under Methven Street and Canal Street may date from Edward III's refortification of the city in 1336.

4

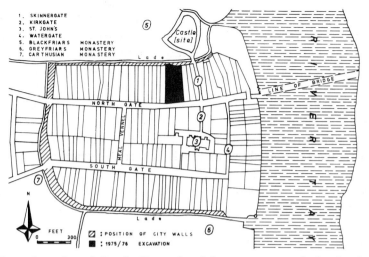

1. SKINNERGATE
2. KIRKGATE
3. ST. JOHN'S
4. WATERGATE
5. BLACKFRIARS MONASTERY
6. GREYFRIARS MONASTERY
7. CARTHUSIAN MONASTERY

Map of medieval Perth (*Reproduced by permission of the Scottish Urban Archaeological Trust*).

of the City Mills hotel foyer. Now much reduced, the lade was said to be 16 feet deep and 20 feet across in the fifteenth century.

Only a few yards away, an extensive work of renovation was recently undertaken on the Lower City Mills—two Victorian mills housed in one building which had, for too long been an unsightly ruin. Once again, visitors could see the stones actually grinding locally grown grain into wholemeal flour and savour the newly baked product in another part of the building which was set aside as a tearoom. Within the same area, the part where the barley used to be ground were also housed various craft work shops. Sadly, the future of this imaginative project is at present in doubt for financial reasons. A short run of the lade is visible before it disappears beneath Mill Street.

With the town walls following the same line just within the lade, the town was now in a state of all-round defence, heightened by a number of watchtowers such as the Spey Tower at the south-east corner of the town. Finally, there was, for a time, a royal castle outside the walls, to which Skinnergate led through the Red Brig Port.* The castle was, as we have suggested, probably little more than an earth work with a timber superstructure, but it did have its own chapel.

If earthwork it was, the site was ill-chosen owing to the Tay's propensity to flooding which proved such a disaster in the year 1209. It had become necessary for King William the Lion to summon his notables to raise money which he had been compelled to promise to the King of England. It was Michaelmas—usually a pleasant enough season in Perth— and it was there that William had chosen. But the weather broke and, as Professor Duncan describes:

> The rain fell in torrents, rivers burst their banks and especially the Tay with the Almond. Destroying a certain 'mountain', it carried away various houses, the bridge, and the old chapel. King William and his brother sailed out of the town in a very little boat seeking dry land, and with them a very few of the magnates who were present. Other magnates who were in the town saved themselves as best they could, either in little boats or in the solars, the upstairs rooms of the burgesses. Then the tide turning began to rise and the swollen river far from getting away, surged through the streets of the town so that not only cobbles and boats but big ships could sail freely through streets and open places.†

Many have been the later floods and many the devices undertaken to minimise their effects over the subsequent centuries but the whole of the North Inch was under water as recently as 1990 and 1993 and many thousands of pounds had to be spent on making good the damage in the area.

This then was the extent of the burgh, but nothing remains today of such buildings as the Kings might have seen. There was a church, but not the cathedral-sized St John's Kirk; the earliest fragments of that, impressive as they are, only date from the fifteenth century. One cannot even be certain that the earlier church stood on the same spot, but it is extremely likely. Nor can one be sure that the High Street (or 'North

---

*A word of explanation is due here. 'Gate' in old Scots is a street, whereas what we mean by a gate in the wall is a 'Port' from the Latin *porta*.
†Professor A.A.M. Duncan in a lecture delivered to the Perthshire Society of Natural Science, 24 March 1973.

Central Perth from the air, c. 1970 (Reproduced by Courtesy of Perthshire Tourist Board).

Gate' to give it its original name) followed exactly its modern line, but it clearly developed from the Watergate and consisted of the workshop-dwellings of craftsmen. South Street developed later and never was as fashionable as the High Street; as late as 1800 it was described as having very mean properties along it as compared with the High Street and, especially the latter's eastern, earlier end. It was here that the Council House was built and the prison; here that justice was administered and commercial dues paid.

Outside the walls, no doubt because of the nuisance caused by the smells, were the tanneries reached by the Skinnergate.

In its early days, more merchandise passed through Perth than through any other Scottish city, and, for even longer, Perth's trade was second only to Berwick-on-Tweed. And as a centre of administration, more royal charters were issued from Perth and Scone than from anywhere else at the beginning of the fourteenth century. Local products such as wool, hides and salmon were exported—luxury goods imported.

That much external trade should be concentrated here, did not in any way hold back the prosperity of local craftsmen, especially where it was not necessary to go far afield for raw materials. There was a plentiful supply of hides to provide work for the tanners who served the glovers and the loriners (makers of harness) and the soutars (shoemakers). Horn, too, was plentiful from both wild and domestic animals and was fashioned into spoons and other implements requiring handles. Such trades have been enshrined in the names of streets such as Skinnergate and Horners Lane and Baxters Vennel.*

Exciting discoveries have recently been made by archaeologists digging in areas left vacant for a time while sites have been cleared for development. In 1975–6 Marks and Spencers moved to larger premises in the High Street and they made more than a year available for research so that a late sixteenth century tower house known as the Old Parliament House

---

*Vennel (from the French): a passage way; only found in one other Scottish town—Dumfries.

Reconstruction of a medieval street (*Reproduced by permission of the Scottish Urban Archaeological Trust*).

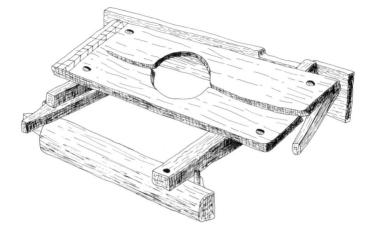

A medieval wooden toilet seat from Kirk Close (*Reproduced by permission of the Scottish Urban Archaeological Trust*).

could be excavated. (Several Parliaments did meet in Perth over the years but there is no evidence that they met in this particular building). In the damp soil, much organic material had survived in the way of leather and textiles that would have perished in most soils.

The Interim Report notes the large amount of fragments of pottery retrieved, chiefly local, but some from further afield and comments on:

> The variety of metal objects found, including iron, bronze, lead, pewter, gold and silver illustrating different aspects of life in mediaeval Perth. Everyday objects such as knives, nails, pins, barrel locks and tools like spades are all represented. Sometimes the knives even have their wooden handles intact. Other aspects, such as personal adornment, are also well illustrated by a number of decorated pins, buckles, buttons and a series of ring-brooches of varying sizes and materials. Nevertheless it was perhaps the more exotic finds, such as the ampulla (holy water flask), which some pilgrim brought back from Canterbury within a few years of Becket's death, and the finely decorated prick spur which have perhaps best shown how well-developed Perth's trade and cultural connections already were by the time of William the Lion. The spur is a fine example of Romanesque work; and it is perhaps significant that Baldwin the Lorimer, a

Fleming who made trappings for the King's horses, was granted a property near the city during David I's reign.

For all that, it must have been the finds of perishable organic origin that would have normally disintegrated that must have given greatest pleasure because of their rarity and because such articles can with modern techniques now be preserved and displayed. Complete shoes and boots were found, as were a number of decorated knife sheaths and belts.

Since then, further excavations have taken place in the High Street; in the Meal Vennel, once an important transverse street joining the High Street to South Street; elsewhere within the confines of the encircling lades; and even outside

Child's leather shoe from Perth High Street excavations, 1975 (*Reproduced by permission of Perth and Kinross District Council Museums and Art Galleries Department, Scotland*).

11

the mediaeval confines to the west where the Whitefriars had their buildings. The result have been summarised in a booklet prepared by the Scottish Urban Archaeological Trust obtainable (amongst other places) from the Perth & Kinross District Libraries for £1.50 and a 'must' for any citizen or visitor who wants to know what mediaeval Perth must have looked like; what sort of frail houses the people lived in; what they ate, and how they worked. It is as beautifully illustrated as it is clearly and informatively written.

The High Street itself was broad enough, but a mere trackway, gravelled over but without firm foundation or binding surface, muddy in the wet season, dusty when it was dry. The little homes on either side of the street measured often no more than 4m by 3m, to house a family and often take in animals too; 'grim, dark, cold, dirty and crowded' and, to judge by the lack of lamps found, probably quite unlit after dark. Earth floors strewn with straw cannot have been conducive to clean living nor elementary thatching to the exclusion of the elements, while both must have harboured every kind of insect. Upright posts formed the skeleton of the walls, filled in with wattle—hardly adequate insulation against the Perthshire winter. Internal hearths, whether for warmth or for cooking, would have been inefficient as well as the highest possible fire risk.

By and large, these houses stood each in its own little toft or plot running at right angles to the main street, offering space for a few hens or some kale, and also for the disposal of rubbish in pits. Such middens, say the report, give clues as to the prevailing diet:

> Animal bone is particularly durable and therefore much evidence is gained by identifying the species present. Cattle and sheep or goats were the most common but pigs and game, such as deer and hare were also eaten. The bones of domestic fowl have also been found as well as egg shells. Bones of cod and salmon have been recovered and shellfish such as oysters and mussels were also eaten. The plant material is normally identified from surviving seeds. . . . including wheat, oats and barley. Turnip seeds were found and it is known that peas and beans were imported into Scotland in the 13th century, but

they do not survive well. Hazelnuts were especially common and seeds of local fruits such as apples, blackberries and strawberries were eaten and well over 1,000 blackberry seeds were found in the cesspit from Kirk Close.
    Most of the cooking was done over open fires and bread was baked in clay ovens.

Plenty of ceramic remains showed that cooks were not short of containers for storage or for cooking, but for eating, small knives, horn spoons and wooden platters were favoured:
    There was, of course, no sanitation to speak of; no organised refuse collection; no sewer. The smell must have been appalling and all-pervasive. Yet one of the most unexpected finds (in Kirk Close) was that one of these small hovels harboured an internal latrine. It was made up of a timber-lined pit with a crudely carved but modern-looking toilet seat. And in its surviving fill were many pieces of moss which was the medieval equivalent of toilet paper.

CHAPTER TWO

Perth's Early Troubles

If the Kings and their courts brought prosperity to the burgh, they also ensured that the burgh suffered more than it would have wished during the unquiet times which followed the disputed succession of the thirteenth century and the consequent invasions of the English. Edward I was said to have slaughtered seventeen thousand when he sacked Berwick; Perth, forewarned, managed to escape a like fate. At his first entry, Edward was able to celebrate the Feast of the Nativity of St John the Baptist 'with circumstances of high feudal solemnity, regaling his friends, creating new knights, and solacing himself'. No doubt a jolly time was had by all but, on his return south, Perth suffered the humiliation of seeing the Stone of Destiny and much else removed. And, from 1296, Perth was not long free of fighting as, in turn, Wallace and then Bruce strove to evict the English.

Marshall, in his *Historic Scenes in Perthshire*, preserves a delightful if improbable story of Wallace's ruse to avoid an expensive assault on its lades and walls (which Edward had ordered to be strengthened). On a reconnaissance, Wallace is said to have fallen in love with 'a fair damsel of the Fair City' whom he visited in the disguise of a priest; saw his mistress; and arranged to be with her again in three days time. In spite of his caution, certain enemies observed him and immediately gave information to Sir Gerard Heron and Sir James Butler, who held the town for the English. The woman was called before them and at first denied any knowledge of Wallace; but threatened, on the one hand, with being burned if she did not reveal all she knew, and promised, on the other, great riches and honour and marriage to a knight, if she disclose it, the temptation was too great for Delilah's virtue. She agreed to betray her Samson to the Philistines. Wallace kept his appointment with her but refused to stay overnight with her;

and it was during the night that he was to be betrayed. Suspecting that her paction with his enemies was discovered, fear overwhelmed her; and, closely questioned by her gallant, she confessed what she had done and threw herself on his mercy. Believing her contrition to be sincere he forgave her, and borrowing part of her attire as a disguise, he hurried away by the south gate. To the many armed men he found there, he dissembled, telling them to hurry to the chamber of the leman, where, he said, Wallace would be found, locked in. Misled by this information, he was allowed to pass without further question, and he hurried on with such strides as awakened the suspicions of some soldiers, who followed him as far as the South Inch, where, turning on them, he slew the two foremost of his pursuers and escaped, only to return next year to achieve his aim by a carefully planned and well organised assault. Two subsequent sieges he managed to fend off before the tide turned against him as the more powerful of those who should have supported him failed to come in and he was betrayed by Sir John Monteith. Edward, most unjustly had him tried as a rebel (though he had never sworn allegiance to any Englishman) and barbarously executed. After the division of his limbs, his right leg and foot were sent to Perth to be displayed as a warning. Two years later, Edward I himself was dead, and, with the much less able Edward II, the way was clear for Bruce.

Not that even he was, at first, successful. Before he could be seen to have royal authority, he must be formally seated on the Stone of Scone by the Earl of Fife, but the Stone was gone and the Earl was in Edward's hands, and his sister's husband was a partisan of the Red Comyn whose slaying Bruce had yet to live down. For all that he managed to assemble those who were ready to back him in the neighbourhood of Scone in 1306. And there, with the somewhat surprising blessing of the Archbishop of Glasgow and the even more daring appearance of the Countess of Buchan, a circlet of gold, made for the occasion, was placed on his head by the Countess, who suffered dearly for her action when she was later captured by the English.

Even so there was a long, hard way to go. The eviction of Edward's garrison commander in Perth, the Earl of Pembroke, was his first priority, but Bruce was outwitted and then defeated. On a Sabbath day he had sent a challenge to Pembroke to sally forth and meet him on open ground to which the latter replied that he would do so on the morrow. Bruce rashly accepted his word and withdrew to Methven, only to be followed up, that evening, by Pembroke, who caught him completely unprepared and put his five hundred men to flight. Bruce had to go into hiding and for some time was little more than a guerilla and constantly on the run. It is of that time that the many stories are told such as that of his despairingly watching the persistence of a spider.

One disaster followed another. His wife and his daughter, on their way to safety, were captured and kept prisoner. The young Countess of Buchan whose dash to the coronation of Bruce had caused the English court to accuse her of being his mistress, and Mary Bruce, whose husband, Sir Neil Campbell, was still in arms with her brother, were the objects of Edward's greatest displeasure. For these ladies, he ordered that wooden cages should be built jutting from the battlements of Berwick and Roxburgh castles respectively, so that they should be shut up like animals in a zoo, exposed to the gaze of passers by with the only concession to their modesty the provision of privies within the walls. A similar plan for Bruce's daughter who was only twelve was abandoned on account of her youth and she was sent to a nunnery instead. Two of Bruce's brothers were killed. But all this happened far from Perth which could not be retaken until the relentless Edward's powers began to fail; its oppressed citizens must have prayed earnestly for his death.

When, at last, the tide began to turn and Bruce was able to evict the English troops from most of the castles that they had garrisoned, Bruce made his way from the south-west to Perth but a six-week siege of the city, the walls of which had been considerably strengthened, achieved little, and a combination of stratagem and personal daring was called for. At New Year 1312, he appeared to have abandoned the siege and marched his forces away. Just one week later he returned on a grimly dark January night, with a picked body of men equipped with scaling ladders. He led them through the waters of the lade which reached to their necks. He personally was the second to mount his ladder and take the garrison by surprise, over-confident that their defences were impregnable.

There followed the triumph of Bannockburn, the capture of Stirling Castle and the gradual establishment of his rule throughout the whole kingdom. There is no evidence that Bruce felt any particular warmth toward Perth itself, as several of his successors did; indeed he ordered its defences to be razed to the ground (later to be rebuilt by Edward III). But he did require the abbot of Scone to provide stone for the repair of St John's Kirk and for a bridge over the Tay, though it is doubtful whether anything stronger was achieved than a wooden structure at the time. And, like all Scottish kings he had to visit the burgh from time to time to hold Parliaments and issue charters and, above all to consume his rents which were paid in kind, and collect his dues on the commerce passing through the port. His chosen physician, Magister Malvinus, lived in Perth and visits were needed because of the skin troubles from which he suffered—at one time claimed to be leprosy but more probably scurvy. He also hired a 'house' for his captive lion, the cost of whose food is recorded in the royal accounts as being £6, 13s and 4d. Its cage and its keeper's wages were paid by the costumers of Perth.

On his death in 1329, his son and successor David was only five years old but that did not prevent a fully ceremonial coronation at Scone, two years later, once more an expense for the burgesses, who had to contribute towards the festivities a boar and five dozen lampreys. Nor did David's later reign contribute anything in return. John Balliol's eldest son managed to invade Scotland once again to renew the civil wars and, in the course of them, the city changed hands more than once. The burgesses had also, like the rest, to contribute towards a large ransom for a king to whom they had little reason to be grateful. On top of that, they suffered serious loss as a result of a visitation of the plague. Nor, when David died

The North Inch, seen from across the River Tay.

in 1371 was there any great improvement in spite of the fact that Robert II did regard Perth as his favourite place of residence. He had not achieved anything outstanding while he was acting as Regent and, now that he was King himself, he was nearly seventy—a great age for those days—and failing. And his son and heir was of little help, for he had never fully recovered from being kicked by a horse in his youth. That is the only excuse one can make for him allowing the best known event in Perth's whole history.

That the King deliberately encouraged the idea of the Battle of the Clans, I cannot believe. Nothing has come down to us to suggest that he was the sort of man who would take a sadistic delight in arranging—and personally watching—sixty men hack each other to death, as if he were a Roman Emperor. It was a plot hatched up by two of his earls whom he had commissioned to end centuries of feuding between the Northern factions, of Clans Chattan and Kay, according to Sir Walter Scott, though Professor Mackie substitutes Cameron for Kay.

The Earls proposed (and the antagonists accepted) that a

18

suitable way to end the feuding would be by a sort of mass trial by combat after the feudal judicial manner. Thirty champions were to be chosen by each side who were to fight in an enclosure on the North Inch of Perth in the presence of the King; body armour and shields were disallowed and only weapons of offence were to be used, and so a fight to the death was obviously envisaged. For the greater comfort of the Court, £14 25s 11p was spent on a stand, erected, it may be said, on land that should have been regarded as sacred—the grounds of the Blackfriars. October 25, 1396, was named as the day and lusting spectators came from as far afield as England. Written records of the details do not survive but enough lived on in oral tradition to give the author of the Waverley novels his set piece for *The Fair Maid of Perth*, as Marshall summarises:

> Just as the combat was about to begin, some delay unexpectedly took place. It was discovered that the heart of one of the Clan Chattan had failed him, and that, throwing himself into the Tay, he had swum across it, and fled with a whole skin to his native mountains. Proclamation having been made for one to take his place, Henry o' the Wynd, an armourer of the city whom Sir Walter Scott has rescued from the oblivion into which most of Harry's contemporaries have sunk, offered his services. Springing within the barriers, he said, 'Here am I: will anyone fee me to engage with these hirelings in this stage play? For half a mark will I try the game; provided I stay alive, I have my board of one of you so long as I live.' The offer was gladly accepted.

The number of the devoted sixty being thus made complete, the signal was given to them to engage in mortal combat. The onset was terrific; and the yells and the butchery as the hand to hand struggle proceeded must have made all ears tingle, all eyes grow dim, all hearts to melt. As they fought with the two-handed sword and the axe, the wounds they inflicted on each other were of a ghastly size and character. Heads were cloven asunder, limbs were lopped from the trunk. The meadow was soon drenched with blood and covered with dead and wounded men; and they clashed and mangled and destroyed each other, till only one of the Clan Kay remained alive. Eleven of Clan Chattan survived; but they were so severely wounded that not one of them was able to follow the single remaining opponent who made his escape by plunging into the Tay and swimming to the other side. The Perth armourer performed prodigies of valour and contributed to the victory of the clan to which he had attached himself but tradition says that when the battle was over, he could not tell which was the clan he had fought for, but answered that he 'was fechting for his ain hand'!

Accounts differ as to whether the North was any more peaceful as a result of this fearful blood-letting.

At any rate it was not long before another crime was committed in Perth, on the same site and this time actually within the walls of the Blackfriars monastery itself, and on the person of the King. Robert III's son and successor James I, had moved too fast and in an arbitrary way in order to try to achieve a more peaceful Scotland for his subjects. He declared that 'if God give me life, though it be but the life of a dog, then throughout Scotland, with His help, will I make the key keep the castle and the bracken bush the cow.' Every man was to have a chance to follow his own business in peace and unoppressed. Not surprisingly he made enemies amongst those who for too long had been the oppressors, amongst whom were his own uncle, James Stewart, Earl of Atholl, and Atholl's son, and Patrick Graham of Kincardine. These conspirators, knowing that the king was at his favourite residence obtained access, one February night, to the Blackfriars monastery. Bursting into the King's chamber they found he was not there; he had had just enough warning to hide in a drain beneath the floor boards but could not get to freedom that way because he had recently given orders for the drain to be blocked because he had lost too many tennis balls down it . . . When the murderers returned, a lady-in-waiting gallantly tried to keep the chamber door closed against them by thrusting her arm though the sockets of the bars intended to keep the door barred but her arm was all too easily broken. James killed two men in his own defence but was struck down by Graham who denied him even the solace of the confessor for whom he asked. James himself had often been harsh in the punishments he exacted. They were nothing to those imposed by the Queen who had been forced to witness her husband's death and had, indeed, been wounded herself. She had Atholl tortured for two days before he was disembowelled on the third. Graham was nailed naked to a pillar and then pulled to pieces with pincers.

It is not surprising that, for a while, Kings were seen rather less often in Perth and, indeed, the time was coming when the burgh would increasingly have to take second place to Edinburgh both in commerce and as a centre of government. Scotland was to have a true Capital at last.

With the Kings less prominent, we begin to read of locally born men coming to the fore. Hal o' the Wynd may be something of a legend but with the rise of the family of Mercer we come on four-square historical persons who rose to riches through their own energies and enterprise and personal daring; traded abroad; and eventually represented their country as ambassadors both in England and on the Continent. But we shall treat of them in the following chapter for it is time to take a walk round the bounds of mediaeval Perth to appreciate its smallness and its compactness. There were as yet hardly anyone except the monks and friars who lived outside the city walls but a few artisans worked outside, to make use of the water power of the lades just to the west of the walls.

CHAPTER THREE

A Walk Round the Bounds of Medieval Perth

It would seem appropriate to start at the foot of the High Street. Here is a house—admittedly not a very old one—bearing the arms of the first well-documented commoner family to belong to the burgh, that of the Mercers to whom it once belonged. Here too, on your left, is the Watergate, the oldest of all Perth's streets, serving as it did the little boats that could make their way up the Tay; it was the nucleus of the town and soon contained the first stone-built houses for those grandees of the neighbourhood who wanted a town residence to complement their fortified but not necessarily warm or convenient castles, as well as for those more successful of the merchants who wanted to have the same grandeur. Here, where you are standing, stood the ancient Tolbooth blocking the end of the street, the place of customs, the jail and the adjoining Council House, which in its various rebuildings has never moved far from its original position. But a huge effort of the imagination is needed to recapture the mediaeval view.

Tay Street, with its lovely riverside outlook, has got to be imagined away. All the land back as far as the great dwellings of the Watergate was garden or open space down to the river's edge. And, inland of the Watergate there was no St John Street as yet; while, if you look to the right, not only Tay Street but George Street, too, must go; Skinnergate would have been the first transverse walkway; it connected St John's Kirk, via the narrow Kirkgate, to the Red Brig Port (Gate) outside of which stood the castle and the Skinners' yards. These lands later passed to the Blackfriars and are now covered by the large car park behind the Museum and Art Gallery.

To return to the Watergate, where families such as those of the Earls of Gowrie, of Erroll and of Kinnoull had their mansions as, eventually did the Mercers and the Sandemans. Today it has fallen on evil times and the only things worth seeking out are an old doorway which bears the date 1725 (at the back of Timothy's restaurant premises) with, next to it, the entrance to the former Hall of the Incorporation of Wrights; their sign may be seen over the door. They were the workers with edged tools, joiners and wheel-wrights.

Once upon a time, the glory of the Watergate—and of Perth—was Gowrie House which was only pulled down at the beginning of the last century to make way for the Sheriff Court and the County Hall. It was a turreted mansion ranging

The former Gowrie House, Perth. An engraving by W. H. Lizars, after Robert Gibb (1801–37) (*Reproduced by permission of Perth and Kinross District Council Museums and Art Galleries Department, Scotland*).

round three sides of a square. Originally built in 1520 by a Countess of Huntly, it then passed to the ill-fated family of Ruthvens, Earls of Gowrie, who were involved in two attempts to gain power in Scotland by securing possession of the person of James VI. The first was when they kidnapped him while he was still a boy in 1582 and held him briefly at Huntingtower—a treason for which the Ist Earl was executed. Later, in 1600, the Master of Gowrie, brother to the 3rd Earl, lured the credulous James from Falkland, where he was pursuing his favourite occupation of hunting, to Gowrie House on the pretext of introducing him to a man with a wonderful pot of gold. James, separated from his own attendants after supper, was heard to shout from one of the towers 'I am murdered! Treason! Treason! Help! Help!' His courtiers rushed to his side and both the Master and his brother (who may have known less of what was going on) were quickly dispatched. It is only fair to add that so convenient was it for James to have the Ruthvens out of the way that many of his contemporaries, (and others since) believed that the whole business was planned by James himself. But it is hardly credible because the King was a notoriously timorous man; not at all the sort who would risk his own person as a bait.

At the corner of the Watergate and the High Street, the Georgian façade of the Prudential Assurance Company is worth noticing. At one time it was a home of the Mercer family and it bears, high up, their arms—a stork with a snake or an eel in its mouth and three mill rhynds (the cross-shaped fittings to support a millstone)—referring to an ancient tradition that they had gifted the city's mills to King Malcolm Canmore 1057–93. (Malcolm's descendant Robert III certainly gifted them back to the burgh.) Another tradition tells of a bargain by which the Mercers presented to Perth the open spaces of the North and South Inches in return for which they were to receive the right to burial within the walls of St John's Kirk, giving birth to the rhyme:

> Folk say the Mercers tried the town to cheat
> When for two inches they did gain six feet.

We are on surer ground when, in the fourteenth century, one

24

Huntingtower, formerly Ruthven Castle.

of the family was well enough established to be the Provost and enough of a benefactor to be allowed to appropriate the north transept of the Kirk for their family vault. Their hatchment still hangs there. Other members of the family established themselves at Meikleour (where they still live), at Aldie and at Gorthie. And by the nineteenth century they had replaced the Ruthvens at Huntingtower which they later presented to the nation. Just outside Perth, to the west, it has some very fine painted ceilings and is well worth a visit. It has also a charming if improbable legend which we owe to Pennant who heard it when he visited the castle in 1769:

> A daughter of the 1st Earl of Gowrie was addressed by a young gentleman of inferior rank, a frequent visitor of the family, who would never give the least countenance to his suit. His lodging was in the tower separate from that of his mistress. The lady, before the doors were locked, conveyed herself thither into her lover's apartment; but some prying duenna acquainted the Countess with it; who, cutting off as she thought, all possibility of retreat, hastened to surprise them. The young lady's ears were quick; she heard the footsteps of the old Countess, ran to the top of the leads and took the desperate leap of 9 feet 4 inches over a chasm of sixty feet, and luckily landing on the battlements of the other tower, crept into her own

bed, where her astonished mother found her, and, of course, apologised for the unfounded suspicion. The fair daughter did not choose to repeat the leap; but, next night, eloped and was married to her lover.

The castle is open to the public.

Another merchant family which, at one time, had a home in the Watergate was that of the Sandemans. They were originally concerned in the bleaching trade before they became internationally famed for importing Portuguese wines to replace those of France which had become our enemy under Napoleon. When their new venture required George Sandeman to move to London, he wrote that he would never lose his affection for his childhood home and he contributed generously to the foundation of the new Academy. Another member of the same family donated the Sandeman Library.

Back in the High Street, and between the Watergate and Skinnergate used to stand the town's Mercat Cross. This was

The Edwardian Mercat Cross.

pulled down by Cromwell in 1651, along with other valued buildings and many of the memorials from the Greyfriars Burial ground, to build his Citadel on the South Inch. After the Restoration of Charles II, a second cross was erected by Sir Patrick Threipland of Fingask, when he was Provost in 1667, which, from its description, must have been very like that of Edinburgh. Prince Charles Edward had his father proclaimed as James VIII from it in 1745 but the cross did not long survive that moment of glory, for, twenty years later, the city fathers decided that it was proving an obstruction and sold it for £5.2.6d. In taking it down, it was damaged but the Threipland family managed to retrieve the stone column on which had stood a unicorn's head. They have retained possession of it ever since and it has stood (with a new head) at Fingask except for the years 1917–68 when the Threiplands were at Dale House, Halkirk. The Council eventually placed a new cross in St John's Square as a memorial to Edward VII. Modern though it is, it does keep alive some of the ancient traditions by incorporating the insignia of the medieval crafts.

Its original site, at the river end of the High Street became, after the Watergate, the fashionable locality. Lord Stormont had a town house here on the north side where the Bank of Scotland has a branch and he gave hospitality to the Young Pretender in 1745. That house has gone but, near where it stood, an old doorway survives at No. 15 with a typical dog-legged close (or alley) behind it. The date over the entrance is 1699, in which year Robert Graham, Town Clerk, and a member of a family closely connected with the neighbourhood married Elizabeth Cunningham. It is adorned with their initials and the scallop shells and the roses of the Grahams of Gorthie. The head represents that of the executed Marquess of Montrose.

From here we take not George Street which only dates from the late eighteenth century, but the medieval route of the Skinnergate, past the Ship Inn which stands on the site of an older hostelry, and the lodging house for men built by yet another family of Perth benefactors, the Dewars, across the car park where the castle once stood to the 'Fair Maid's

The Fair Maid's House.

House'. This has been much restored but still presents a
medieval aspect with, alongside it, the frontage of a property
lived in by Lord John Murray from 1755-87 when he was
Member of Parliament for Perthshire. Although the Fair
Maid's House stands outside the town defences, its ancient
appearance served to appeal to Sir Walter Scott who rendered
it famous as the dwelling of his hero Simon the Glover and
his daughter Catherine, the Fair Maid herself. It has, at any
rate, a genuine Glover connection in that it was the meeting
place of the Incorporation from 1629-1787. As such, the
niche above the doorway is more likely to have held a statue
of St Bartholemew (their patron) than the curfew bell featured
in the novel. The house was certainly conveniently situated
near to the tanning yards and accessible by the Skinnergate.
After being used for a time as a cabinet maker's workshop, it
was eventually largely rebuilt and is now part craft shop and

part picture gallery. Other interesting things about it may be read on a plaque there.

When Charles I visited Perth in 1633, it was the Incorporation of Glovers who were chosen to provide entertainment for him. While he sat in a chair by the river's edge, in the grounds of Gowrie House, thirteen of their number danced a Morris Dance for him on a raft. Their pale green dresses must have been extremely expensive, slashed and beribboned as they were and each ornamented with 252 small circular bells. The contemporary minute in their records declares:

15th June, 1633.—Which day our dread Sovereign, Charles I, King of England, France and Ireland—'being accompanied with the Nobilitie of Scotland ryding behind him'—desired out of his gracious favour to visit his own city of the burgh of Perth upon the 8th day of July, and come to his own lodging, went down to the garden thereof, His Majestie's chair being set upon a wall thereof next to the

The Glover's Dance Dress, by J. C. Howie. Watercolour and ink (*Reproduced by permission of Perth and Kinross District Council Museums and Art Galleries Department, Scotland*).

Tay, where upon was ane falt stage of timber clead with birks upon the which for His Majestie's welcome and entry. Wheirupon thirteen of our brethren of this our calling of Glovers, with green caps, silver strings, reiid ribbons, white shoes, with bells about their leigs, schering raper in their hands, and all other abulziment, danced our sword dance with many difficult knots and allafallajessa, five being under and five above upon their shoulders, three of them dancing through their feet, drinking wine and breaking glasses about them (which God be praised wis acted without hurt or skaith to any) which drew us to great charges—amounting to the sum of 350 marks—yet not to be remembered (i.e. grudged), because wee was graciously accepted be our Sovereign and both estates to our honour and commendation.

One such dress survives and, after undergoing conservation, may be seen in the Museum today.

Returning to the High Street, No. 68 has one of the older frontages, recently but most successfully restored. It is sad that the same could not have been done in 1908 for the former Guild Hall of the Incorporation of Guilds. Further along, by the side of Woolworths, is Guard Vennel, the way by which the Town Guard who were stationed here would march to the city's walls. Here too once stood the Mint and a house in which the famous General Wolfe stayed while he was still a subaltern; and alongside the theatre is the oddly named Cutlog Vennel. Vennel, like so many Scots words comes from the French. Many of Perth's buildings have a small plate telling what is known of their history.

It has been noticed (in the admirable booklet published by the Town Council—*Walks in Perth*) that one of the features of Perth is the way in which streets do not drift to an untidy end; they finish with interesting views (e.g. South Street) or special terminal buildings such as the Salutation Hotel opposite the end of St John Street and St Leonard's Church at the end of Charterhouse Lane. In the case of the High Street, the focal point was provided deliberately, the octagonal St Paul's Church designed by John Paterson in the Gothic Revival style.*

Opposite is a plain but graceful building which used to

*St Paul's church is no longer used as such and its future remains uncertain.

The Lower City Mills.

house the congregation of the Dissenting Glassites until they ceased to meet in 1929. The Reverend John Glass was deposed from his living at Tealing in 1728 for his anti-Establishment views, and his followers built a meeting house for him on this site when he moved to Perth in 1733. This, in its turn, was replaced by the present structure. The Glassites were a some- what exclusive sect who secured unanimity 'in all proceedings by the simple expedient of expelling any member who obsti- nately differs in any opinion from the majority'. They were also unusual for those days in that they held a weekly Communion service, after which they sat down to a substan- tial dinner, for which they were known as the Kail Kirkers. Another nickname arose from the fact that two daughters of The Rev. John Glass were married to members of the Perth family of Sandeman, one of whom emigrated to the USA and founded a congregation there who were known as Sandemanians. In 1929 the building, later named the Grant Miller Hall, passed to the congregation of St Paul's as their Session House. It is now a centre of aerobics, keepfit, karate and dancing. Behind, in the Mill Wynd, another old frontage associated with Scott's *Fair Maid of Perth*, has been preserved—that of the house chosen by him to be that of the armourer Hal o' the Wynd; it is now part of the back premises of the Clydesdale Bank.

The nearby restoration by the Reo Stakis Organisation of the Upper City Mill to form a hotel won the annual Civic Trust Award Scheme in 1971. It not only preserved the shell but, most cleverly, made a feature of the old wheel which can still be seen beneath a heavy glass panel let into the floor of the foyer. And the old beams of the roof have been left exposed in the hotel ballroom—a magnificent example of a king pin roof.

The refurbishment of the Lower City Mill, described on page five, also won the Civic Award twenty years later, after the District Council had spent £300,000 to create what should surely prove a most attractive tourist attraction. These two mills were built towards the end of the eighteenth century but mills on this site, and driven by the lade, have stood here since earliest times.

None of the ways back to our starting point offers much to see in the way of antiquarian interest or indeed of outstanding modern architecture, though Mill Street, once the site of the burgh's wash-house, has recently been pleasantly tidied up and contains Perth's only remaining cinema, the North Church and a great Victorian factory that once was Pullar's dye-works.

Canal Street, once the southern boundary of the town, covers another branch. Now it houses a multi-storey car park and a night club, but at its western end has a few pleasant little shops including a saddler's and a picture-framer's, with, on the other side of the road, a dignified building that was once a granary.

There was a time at the start of the Industrial Revolution when it seemed as though linen and damask weaving would be the course along which Perth's development would proceed when water power was the easiest and cheapest source of power; but then came steam and proximity to coalfields enabled other towns to outstrip us. Before the introduction of factories there had always been a considerable number of hand loom weavers. They, and the first factories, had lain outside the city walls and it is to this period that New Row belongs. We will go along it to see the second most remarkable building in Perth—the King James VI Hospital, built on the site of a former Carthusian monastery, the only one of its order in Scotland.

In the Middle Ages Perth had four great religious houses, the earliest being that of the Blackfriars (so called from the colour of their robe). This was founded by Alexander II in 1231 and lay near the castle, overlooking the North Inch and the site of the Battle of the Clans.

Next in time came came the Carmelites or Whitefriars in 1262, to the west of the city in Tullylumb—the smallest of the four.

The Carthusians, whose members also wore a white robe, were an enclosed order of the strictest type. Each monk lived in silence in his own cell—not, as more usually, in dormitory, cloister and refectory. Even on Sundays when there was a common meal, it had to be eaten in silence. James I with his Queen founded it in 1429 and was buried here twelve years later after his untimely murder, as also were his widow and later, Queen Margaret (Tudor), James IV's widow, who had died at her castle of Methven. Unfortunately, the tomb which James I had caused to be made during his lifetime has not survived, nor have those of the two queens.

Last, in order, came the Greyfriars or the Franciscans, whose Friary was south of the city walls at the foot of Speygate. As with the other three, all their buildings are gone but their land was used as a burying ground from 1580 (when it was found that there was no more room in the original area around St John's Kirk) until the nineteenth century. Indeed, for three hundred years it was Perth's only burying ground and it contains many gravestones of great interest, including one from 1580 (*very* early, this) and several before 1652. And, if it had not been for Cromwell's taking stones from it in that year to build his citadel on the South Inch, there would have been many more. Because so many fine examples of grave-stone carvings survive here, Betty Willshire and Doreen Hunter in their fascinating book on eighteenth century Scottish grave-stones have more references to this site than any other, even Edinburgh. Among their illustrations from the Greyfriars are the tombstones of a Hammerman, Patrick Gower 1639, a Glover 1764, a Dyer 1785, a Mariner 1747 with an exceptionally beautiful sailing ship, a Miller 1758, a Mason 1745 and a Barber 1777, each with the appropriate tools of his trade, carved by local craftsmen. There is also a photograph of a large and early stone of 1651, covered with emblems including, not only the shears and iron of the Tailor, but Faith, Hope and Charity and other religious motifs.

The authors modestly state in a footnote that 'there is a new interest in Perth in these memorials and a move afoot to preserve the stones, and spend money on the graveyard there'. As a result, the ground is now, once more, open to visitors at certain times.

In their heyday, the monastic foundations all did good work, preaching, teaching the young, caring for the sick and the poor, and dispensing hospitality to the wayfarer. But, as they became more inward-looking and more concerned with the interests of the wealthy from whom they could hope for further bequests, they increasingly fell from their high ideals until they became that part of the church most violently attacked by the Reformers. An account written of them by a visitor to Perth, just before the Reformation—though satirical—probably contains much truth. He and his companion are supposed to be standing on Kinnoull Hill looking across the river to what were then the city's most conspicuous buildings:

> The warden of the Greyfriars or Franciscan Monastery, that building you see nearest us outside the walls, is well known to be a favourer of the new doctrines. There are but eight of them in that huge house—good canty fellows all of them—known to keep an excellent table, and willing to let all the world alone, so that they are not disturbed at dinner-time. But they are in constant dread of the firebrands in that princely building that you see on the same side of

the town, farther to the west, who can write though their order forbids them to speak. Austere fellows they are, those Carthusians, and pride themselves not a little on this their only establishment in Scotland and on the odour they and it are in with the Queen Regent. But, for all their austerity, there are queer stories told of them and the nuns in the convent of St Leonards and the Magdalenes, both of which are a short distance to the southwards. Certain jolly skippers too, from the coast, under cover of a few oysters or haddocks, wink and glance knowingly at this monasterium vallis virtutis, as the monks call it, while they hint about the many and good ghostly customers they have in Perth. Then there are those Dominicans—beggars they profess themselves to be, like the Franciscans, and sturdy ones they are. See how comfortably they have set themselves down in that palace you see without the walls on the north side of the town just over by the castle there. Ah, these Blackfriars are your men for the pulpit. If you want a good easy confessor, go to the chapels of St Paul's or St Catherine's you see peering above the trees, on the west side of the town, and there you will find one of the Carmelites or Whitefriars from the Tullilum*, a monastery still further to the west, hid from us by a wood; but if you want a discourse that will keep you quaking for a week, go to the church of the Dominicans. And well worthy it is of a visit—such walls, such aisles, such windows; the gardens too, and the gilten arbour. No wonder our monarchs forsook that old gloomy place (the castle) at the end of the bridge for the sweet arbour and the soft beds of the Blackfriars.

When the monastic houses were dissolved, the Regent Moray, on behalf of the infant King, James VI, decreed that their revenues should be devoted to the care of the sick, and his charter was confirmed by James VI himself in 1587. But no hospital was built, as envisaged, and much of the money was diverted towards the upkeep of the town Kirk.

Eventually, in 1750, the existing King James VI Hospital was built at the cost of £1,614. 10s. 7d. and its cupola was added in 1764 when the then Duke of Atholl donated the clock tower from Nairne House which had been demolished. For a time it did care for the sick and the poor and the orphans until in 1836 the hospital side was transferred to new

---

*Recent excavations have established its exact site at the junction of Riggs Road and Long Causeway but no remains are now visible.

King James VI Hospital.

buildings in County Place and the rest converted into flats. (When a still more modern hospital was called for, and the Perth Royal Infirmary was opened, above Rose Crescent, the County Place hospital was taken over as Council Offices. Now a new conversion is planned for an enlarged Public Library.

By 1977, the King James VI Hospital again required repair and extensive restoration was made possible by grants from the Gannochy Trust and the Exchequer. An interesting short history was printed as a result of a project done by Primary VII Caledonian Road School under the supervision of Miss R. Fothergill from which I quote, by permission, the last paragraph:

> Perhaps most interesting historically within the building is the Meeting Room for the managers of the Hospital. It is a fine pine-panelled room and bears the names of the donors to the Hospital Trust round the walls. The earliest recorded donation is 1587 . . . (and) some of the donors' names are accompanied with the appropriate guild sign, giving an immediate link from the present to the past. It is indeed fitting that a building of such historical and architectural interest has been preserved for us.

From the Hospital we return to South Street via County Place where, at No. 3, the former owner of what was then a private house, honoured Burns by placing a statue that he himself had carved above the front door. Unless you need to shop or to visit the Post Office, there is little need to linger. On the left, just before the Post Office, used to stand the John Knox Free Church of which the Rev. John Buchan was minister at the time when his more famous son was born in 1875. Although Lord Tweedsmuir was later made a Freeman of the city, it is difficult really to claim him as one of her sons because the family left for Pathhead, Kirkcaldy when he was only one year old.

The areas where the medieval tradesmen sold their wares are recalled by names such as Meal Vennel which used to run through to the High Street and, on the right by Ropemakers Close and Fleshers Vennel. The tools of their trade may be seen carved on a house between Cow Vennel and Princes Street. The building itself only dates from 1889 but the sign is reproduced from an earlier one on the same site. The fleshers certainly owned property here.* On the same side of the street lies Horners Lane. In Cow Vennel (through which the citizens would drive their cattle to graze on the South Inch) there is an interesting old external stone staircase, recalling the days when such was the normal entrance to the dwelling part of a home where the groundfloor was used as a workplace or a shop. No. 12, an antique shop, retains an old-fashioned bow window, and on the other side of the street a plaque above No. 31–3 testifies to this site as having been the home of the old Grammar School and then of the town's theatre. Further on still, is the little Fountain Close in which the walls have been decorated with a key to South Street's vennels. On the right is the Greyfriars Burying Ground.

One other building deserves further attention, the Salutation Hotel, with its large yet elegant fanlight above the main

---

*I am indebted for this fact, and for much else, to a most informative pamphlet *What's in a Name?* compiled by the pupils of the Caledonian Road Schools under the guidance of miss Rhoda Fothergill and published by the Perth Civic Trust.

The Salutation Hotel.

window and its Highlanders on either side. There has been an inn here since 1699 and there is a tradition that Prince Charles Edward stayed in it in 1745; indeed the room is still shown, though it is more likely that he stayed at Lord Stormont's house in the High Street. But he certainly made use of the inn because it was reported that the only evidence that could be produced against a certain Colonel Bower, a reputed Jacobite, was that 'he had worn a white cockade and had been seen talking with the Prince Charles Edward at the Salutation Inn'.

We return via St Ann's Lane to visit St John's Kirk, architecturally and historically the most significant building in Perth. In spite of restoration in the nineteenth century and some rebuilding after the First World War, it is essentially the church which was put up between 1440 and 1500. Of course, there had been a church here from earliest times but nothing is known of its size or style. What we do know is that David I alienated its revenues to the rich Abbey of Dunfermline, the great church he built as a memorial to his parents who were buried there. Only a small portion was handed on so that our church had fallen into disrepair by the middle of the fifteenth century and civic pride called for a completely new building that would be worthy of so prosperous a burgh. The year 1440 probably saw a start made on the easternmost part, the choir, and we know that the central tower must have been finished (and much admired) by 1511, because in that year Bishop Elphinstone of Aberdeen, who wanted a tower for his St Machar's Cathedral, stipulated that it should be 'weill and stancheously junyt and hewin as the stepyl and prik of the Kirk of Sanct Johnstun is'. Perth, in past times was often known by the name of its patron saint, St John the Baptist.

For the brief period between its completion and the Reformation the interior must have had a magnificently coloured and ornate look, with its thirty or so altars and their embroidered frontals, countless statues and (probably) stained glass windows. At the Reformation, most of the colour was swept away—and, in due course, the grandeur of the Kirk's proportions, too, when partitions were put up to convert the building into three separate churches. Eventually, after various abortive proposals, drastic surgery was undertaken as Perth and

St John's Kirk.

Perthshire's memorial to those who died in 1914–8. The building was made safe and the original conception of the one worthy burghal church was restored. The Town Council launched the appeal and thanks largely to the energy and generosity of the 1st Lord Forteviot, the money was raised. Equally fortunately, Sir Robert Lorimer, the architect of the National War Memorial in Edinburgh, was available to plan and supervise the work. The Kirk reopened for worship in 1926.

After the Second World War, the eastern end of the choir was restored under the direction of Ian Lindsay to mark the 325th year of the Kirk. Though there is some new work, few would deny that everything is in keeping with the original, and that, to a remarkable degree, harmony has been achieved between the mediaeval Catholic conception of a High Church—almost a cathedral—and the requirements of Protestant and Presbyterian worship.

The exterior is plainer than the interior but is worth looking at before going inside, even though it can no longer be appreciated to the extent that it could have been when it stood on its own, unencumbered by the modern buildings which now press so closely upon it. When first built, it was surrounded by a burial ground and, outside that, only the low booths of traders, especially the Fleshers. To the east, there was no St John Street, only the back ends of the gardens of the houses in the Watergate. To the west, there were not the dwarfing City Halls, and its size would have been that much more impressive.

From the south-east the tracery of the big east window can be seen best; from the north-west, the tower, the eye being led up by Halkerston's tower to the corbelled battlements of the parapet, and the pretty external canopy covering a peal of small bells, to the leaden spire with its pleasing pattern. Three times the lead has been blown off, and three times renewed, the last time in 1767. But it is only when one enters the Kirk that one fully appreciates its grandeur. As Dr W. Douglas Simpson wrote in his brief guide (now no longer in print):

Nothing in its somewhat homely exterior has prepared us for the splendid impression of lofty splendour, the whole cathedral-like aspect of the inside, due mainly to the perfect proportions of the different parts of the building.

It is this general atmosphere which is the chief glory, but there are also many details which are outstanding. Since Dr Simpson wrote, the Friends of St John's Kirk have commissioned a new guide, written by Richard Fawcett, Inspector of Ancient monuments—fuller and more generously illustrated.

The north porch has always been known as Halkerston's Tower. John of that name was the Master of Works for the building of Trinity College, Edinburgh, between 1461 and 1469, and so could well have been connected with St John's too but nothing is known for certain. The vaulting of the roof here, with that of the central tower, is one of the finest things in the church.

In the north aisle is a chapel designed by Lorimer as a War Memorial Shrine to house the Golden Book containing the names of those who were killed in 1914–18. Morris Meredith Williams, a collaborator of Lorimer's in the National War Memorial in Edinburgh, designed the window and also carved the scenes from the life of Christ which decorate Lorimer's oak ceiling in the nave. The bronze statue of St John the Baptist is by a young pupil of Lorimer's, Finandra Bose.

The height and the ribbed vaulting of the central tower are made all the more effective by skilful lighting. The oilette or circular opening in the centre, through which the bells were hoisted into position, has a modern Agnus Dei, the emblem of St John the Baptist; smaller holes in the ribs are for the ropes of the bellringers. The north transept which houses the vault of the Mercer family and the hatchment with their coat of arms, was originally longer, like the south transept but was truncated to widen the road outside. The Incorporated Trades have their pews here carved with their craft signs. The woodwork and that on the pulpit and throughout the choir affirms that carving in wood is still a thriving art.

The choir is not only the oldest part of the Kirk; it is the most ornate and the most beautiful with its slender pillars and

Interior of St John's Kirk (*Reproduced by permission of Dr W. H. Findlay*).

high arches, its clerestory of windows above the arches and its massive oak timbers of the mediaeval roof. Round the easternmost pier on the south side runs an inscription:

johanes: FULLAR: et: UXOR: EJUS; MARIOTA: FOULLAR

Since there was a burgess of that name in the 1440s, it seems likely that he may have paid for this pillar in memory of himself and his wife. Other features to notice are the corbels, the carved projections which held up the Royal Gallery dividing the choir from the nave, and the high-up wooden door giving access to it; the north aisle where there is a tablet commemorating the fact that this was the burying place of the Gowries; and the matrix of one of the few brasses in Scotland; the south choir aisle with the museum containing some of the old bells and the beautiful church plate. In the south transept, facing the craft pews are those for the city magistrates and also a fine painted panel which used to form the front of the Wrights' seat. For a time this left the Kirk and was in the Wrights' Hall; no doubt there were others like it which have sadly perished. The craft signs of the Wrights who included coopers, masons and slaters may also be seen on their banner in the George Street museum.

A number of embellishments were undertaken to mark the 325th anniversary; the communion table was placed beneath the central tower and the chancel screen moved forward to its present position, giving it greater prominence and behind it the John Knox Chapel was further beautified; for these changes the architect was W. Schomberg Scott.

The stained glass windows are the subject of a separate guidebook which gives not only a clockwise tour of the Kirk, window by window, but also a background to the medieval tradition of stained glass, and to the early twentieth-century renaissance of the art, to which the finest of the windows belong. Its best-known exponent was the late Douglas Strachan who 'initiated a technique which ensured the transmission of light by means of sparkling colours, thus giving translucency to the leaded mosaics' and also re-discovered the art of producing certain hues which had been lost. He designed the great east window which shows the crucifixion above and the Last Supper below; in the upper half are also two references to the saint to whom the church is dedicated—St John the Baptist preaching and his baptism of Our Lord. Strachan also made the south transept window depicting the adoration of the Three Wise Men, presenting their gifts of gold and frankincense and myrrh, while a boy from the inn feeds one of their horses.

Second only to Dr Douglas Strachan, at any rate as far as St John's is concerned, are Herbert Hendrie and William Wilson. The former designed the large west window of the Nativity, the Stirton window by the north porch, the Dewar window in the north transept and another in the south transept, the Cowan window with St Andrew and St Columba, and the Freemasons' window.

William Wilson designed the MacNab window in the north-west corner of the nave which shows St Nicholas, the patron saint of children and St Christopher, the patron saint of travellers, and the memorial window to those members of the 6th battalion of the Black Watch who gave their lives in 1939–45. Everyone will have their own preferences among these and the other windows but few will question the pre-eminence of the two Strachan works, especially his east window with its differing shades of purple and blue; and some may agree with the present writer in placing Wilson's next, but Hendrie's west window is certainly an effective foil to the east window and admits the rays of the evening sun.

Two other medieval items have survived which are of special interest; the very delicately wrought fifteenth-century candelabrum which hangs in the north transept and a wooden collection box. The former is of Flemish origin and could have been given to the Kirk by James II's Queen, whose master of works Halkerston was; the latter is believed to be the Offrand Stok which stood upon the altar of St Eloi to receive alms given for the decayed members of the Incorporation of Hammermen. One of their number, Andrew Luff, endowed this altar in 1431. His craft included a wide range of workmen, gold and silversmiths, blacksmiths, armourers, clockmakers and saddlers who certainly go back as far as the reign of David I, because one of them, Baldwin the Loriner (or harness maker) had a booth in Perth then.

Not strictly medieval but old enough to be precious and exceedingly beautiful is the silver. There are four communion cups of which the two oldest were probably not made in the first instance for St John's, nor indeed for use in church. They are the Mary Cup probably made in Nuremburg around 1560—'the finest piece of secular foreign plate in Scotland earlier than 1603'—and another cup from Nuremburg, a little later and plainer. Then, from the early seventeenth century come two English Steeple Cups, so-called from the ornamentation on their lids. Finally, and perhaps most beautiful of all, is a piece of Scottish silver, the Baptismal Basin made by David Gilbert in Edinburgh between 1590 and 1594—quite plain but all the more lovely for that. The lettering (which is later) is, no doubt, an attempt to link it with a tradition that it was given to the Kirk by Charles II—inherently unlikely since Charles cannot have had happy memories of St John's where (a cynical man who was either a High Anglican or already a Roman Catholic) he was made to listen to long Presbyterian sermons when he was a prisoner in Perth in 1650. From the present century are two communion cups and two bread plates designed by the late Alastair Cairncross.

The organ, installed in 1928 was built by Frederick Rothwell & Sons who also built the organ of St George's Chapel in Windsor Castle.

Finally, but not least among the treasures of the church, are its bells, 'one of the very best collections of ancient bells in the whole of Britain'. Eight of them survive from pre-Reformation times—a total more than in any other church in the British Isles. The oldest of them goes back to the time of Bannockburn and is inscribed (in Latin) 'Hail Mary, full of Grace; the Lord is with thee'. This hangs with twelve of the older bells in the external bartizan on the north side of the tower but is no longer in use. Then, in the church museum, is a stand holding a two-hundredweight bell inscribed 'Behold the Lamb of God'—English in origin but appropriate to St John's, and five smaller bells cast at Malines in 1526—again rare—and some later ones. The third group, the beautiful ones which we hear today, whether sounding the quarters and the hour, or playing airs, are housed in the main tower. One is old and weighs 28 cwt 14 lb—more than double the weight of any other existing pre-Reformation bell in Scotland; it is inscribed: 'John the Baptist I am called: the voice of one crying in the wilderness: at Malines Peter Waghevens formed me: Let him be blessed who created all things. 1506'. The thirty-four others are modern, cast by Gillett and Johnston of Croydon and dedicated in 1935. Melville Gray of Bowerswell was the moving spirit behind their acquisition.

Since its consecration in 1242, St John's has seen its share of historic events. Edward I kept St John the Baptist's Day here on 24 June 1296 and rendered thanks for the submission of John Balliol. Wallace, and later also Bruce, no doubt offered their thanks when each in turn managed to retake Perth from the English, but the church had suffered badly in the wars, for Bruce had to get stone from the quarries of Scone Abbey for its repair. The body of Edward III's brother, John of Eltham, rested here when he died in Perth in 1306—and the heart of at least one Scottish king is buried within the walls. But the best remembered of all events is the service at which John Knox preached on 11 May 1551, the occasion generally regarded as being the opening of the Reformation in Scotland; this is how he himself described its consequences:

The multitude was so inflamed, that neither could the exhortation of the preacher, nor the commandment of the magistrate, stay them from destroying the places of idolatry. The manner where of was this: . . . it chanced next day. . . . after the sermon, which was vehement against idolatry, that a priest in contempt would go to the Mass. And, to declare his presumption, he would open up an Altar-piece which stood upon the High Altar. There stood beside certain godly men, and among others a young boy who cried with a loud voice, 'This is intolerable that when God by his word hath plainly damned idolatry, we shall see it used in despite.' The priest hereat offended, gave the child a great blow: who in anger took up a stone, and casting it at the priest did hit the tabernacle and brake down the image; and immediately the whole multitude that was about, cast stones, and put hands to the said tabernacle and to all other monuments of idolatry; which they dispatched before the tent men in the town were advertised (for the most part were gone to dinner). Which noised abroad, the whole multitude convened, not of the gentlemen, neither of them that were earnest professors, but of the rascal multitude, who finding nothing to do in that church, did run without deliberation to the Black and Grey Friars; and not withstanding that they had within them very strong guards kept for their defence, yet were their gates incontinent broken open. The first invasion was upon the idolatry; and thereafter the common people began to seek some spoil; and, in very deed, the Greyfriars was a place so well provided, that unless honest men had seen the same, we would have feared to have reported what provision they had. Their sheets, blankets, bedding and coverings were such as no Earl in Scotland hath finer . . . There were but eight persons in the convent and yet had eight punscheons of salt beef (consider the time of year May XI), wine and beer and ale, and all kinds of victual. . . . in which they were so busy that, within two days, those three great places, to wit the Black and Greyfriars and the Charterhouse monks (a building of Wondrous cost and greatness) were so destroyed that the walls only did remain of these great edifications.

In the next reign, James VI and his wife Anne of Denmark both worshipped in the church, and so did the General Assembly which was induced to pass the unpopular Five Articles of Perth, James's attempt to turn back the tide of the Reformation. Charles I, trying to go even further along the same course, also worshipped here when he came north for his Scottish Coronation—no doubt in an attempt to allay Presbyterian fears. Montrose used the building to lock up his Covenanting prisoners in 1644 and Cromwell used is as a Court House. Another 'Reformation' had its beginnings here in 1732 when the Rev. Ebenezer Erskine preached his sermon against Patronage which led to the First Secession.

Prince Charles Edward, an avowed Roman Catholic, had, like his great-uncle, to listen unwillingly to a Protestant sermon as a matter of policy, but his was preached by an Episcopal divine. And—not least—our present Queen gave thanks here for the first twenty-five years of her reign.

CHAPTER FOUR

Georgian Perth

The seventeenth century had seen something of a decline in the importance and the prosperity of Perth, but, towards the middle of the eighteenth, the city began to share in in the growing wealth of the country as a whole. This was especially evident in agriculture, with the introduction of improved techniques and the wider use of the potato. And the effects were all the more felt in an age when town and country were so closely integrated. And, in any case, as Professor Smout has observed:

> Lawyers prosper when farmers and landowners prosper mainly because a large proportion of their profits come from conveyancing and from disputes about land.

Ministers benefited too, and even schoolmasters. And not only was there a greater demand for education, but also for the consumer goods that were produced by the glovers and the shoemakers and the horners and the smiths and other craftsmen. Much of the raw material was a by-product of stock raising, both local and in the Highlands where there was a boom in the 'black' cattle trade. Even the poorest (with one exception to be noted below) were better off, according to the Minister of nearby Coupar Angus who wrote in the *First Statistical Account* 1793:

> At present few servant lads are to be seen in church without their coats of English cloth, hats on their heads and watches in their pockets. (Forty years before) a watch, an eight day clock, or a tea kettle were scarcely to be met with. At present there are few houses without one or other of these articles; perhaps one half of the families in the parish are possessed of all of them.

He was doubtless exaggerating (and maybe the servant lads who had not got fine clothes preferred to stay away from church) but the general point that he was making was sound enough.

Prospectus Civitatis Perthi ('The prospect of the town of Perth'). An engraving for Captain J. Slezer's book, *Theatrum Scotae*, 1693 *(Reproduced by permission of Perth and Kinross District Council Museums and Art Galleries Department, Scotland).*

New techniques were being introduced in industry, too, especially in the textile crafts, and so long as water was all that was needed to turn the new machinery, Perth was well placed. New companies were formed such as the Mill Wynd Company and the New Row Manufacturing Company to cope with the transition from purely domestic to factory weaving of linen first, and later of cotton. In this, and in the allied trades of bleaching and dyeing, not only the merchants but local magnates, such as the Earl of Kinnoull and General Lord Lynedoch, hastened to invest. Roads were improved and more used and, at last, a substantial bridge over the Tay was completed; many trades were helped, in particular, in those days of horse traffic, the blacksmiths, members of the Incorporation of Hammermen. At one time there was work for over thirty of them and even a few years ago there were two such firms with five consecutive generations of the same family in control. Another firm founded at this time and operating for over two hundred years was that of Norwells. Henry of that name must have been learning his trade for several years before he set up on his own as a shoemaker in the High Street. In 1801 he took in his son John whose three sons followed on, and then *their* sons, so that by 1880 the office-bearers of their Incorporation read: Deacon, David Norwell; Boxmaster, John Norwell; Officer, James Norwell. In due course, the surviving Peter Norwell was seventh in line but also, sadly, was the last when he retired.

When lawyers and ministers flourish, so do printers and booksellers. Robert Morison (1722–91) combined both these trades with the office of Postmaster and, like the Norwells, founded a dynasty. Two of his sons (and later his grandsons) followed on, and one of them was instrumental, with the Rev. J. Scott, in founding The Perth Literary and Antiquarian Society, which included among its patrons the eccentric Earl of Buchan; Walter Scott accepted honorary membership and John Galt was a corresponding member. Both the Society and the printing trade still flourish in Perth. The Morisons were also responsible for the Tory *Perthshire Courier*, which, in its earlier days, used to indulge in a good deal of mud slinging with its more radical rival, the still thriving *Perthshire Advertiser*.

Increased prosperity brought about a sharp increase in population with a consequent expansion beyond the medieval boundaries and the development of two elegant suburbs (as they then were) to the north and to the south. In this respect, and in others, Perth was fortunate in having some energetic and able men in charge of her destinies—especially two Provosts, Thomas Marshall (died 1788) and his more famous son, Thomas Hay Marshall to whom the grateful citizens later erected the building which now houses the Museum and Art Gallery, and carries on it a statue of him by a local sculptor called Cochran.

The Marshalls were members of a small group of families who, at this time, entirely monopolised the government of the burgh—an oligarchy known to their opponents (the one section of the community who were not sharing in the growing prosperity—the handloom weavers) as the 'The Beautiful Order'. If you were not a Robertson or a Sandeman, a Fechney, Stewart, Duncan, Ramsay, Caw, Allison or a Marshall, you had little chance of becoming Provost. Mostly such families burnt themselves out after a generation or two, but the Stewarts retained their position for an entire century and the Sandemans for even longer. Their family alone of the Beautiful Order were represented on the first popularly elected Council after the reforms of 1833.

Up till then, the Beautiful Order had monopolised all the more profitable commercial enterprises; it had directed the administration of the burgh and made its bye-laws; it had also kept strictly to itself the judicial function in all petty matters. Their power as magistrates were wielded in a high-handed way. They kept the peace, but in an informal and rough-and-ready manner sometimes through absentmindedness, but sometimes also through partiality. The radical writer Penny has two good stories, the first is about the kindly Provost Marshall senior and concerns a notorious neer-do-well, Perry Mitchell:

> Perry was long a nuisance about the town. He was frequently

apprehended for petty offences. On one of these occasions he was committed to prison; and, when one of the town officers informed old Provost Marshall of it, he exclaimed 'Filthy body, we are continually plagued with him; he deserves a good whipping'. On this, the officer went straight to the jailer and told him that Provost Marshall had ordered Perry to be whipped. The hangman was brought, the accused was stripped and brought downstairs. By this time the thing had taken wind and a crowd had assembled. Provost Marshall, whose shop was below the Skinnergate, seeing the multitude, asked the reason. Someone replied that Perry Mitchell was about to be whipped through the town. The astonished Provost instantly made his way through the multitude, and arrived just in time to rescue Perry from the hands of the hangman.

Incidentally, the Perth hangman had, by this time, ceased to carry out hangings or even serious whippings; when one such had to take place during his period of office, Provost Marshall wrote to his colleague of Edinburgh to borrow the Edinburgh hangman.

Penny was less indulgent in reporting a case in which favouritism was flagrant:

Baillie Allison was sitting judge, when a boy was brought before him for a practice, very common at the time, of getting up to the steeple from the roof of the church . . . the object being to swing by the bell ropes . . . This boy, the son of a poor widow, was caught in the act . . . and Baillie Allison sentenced him to two months confinement. . . . but the boy hesitated to leave the court. 'Take him away' was called out by the Baillie, rather in a pet at the culprit not obeying the order. In reply to which, the boy asserted that there were others present equally involved who ought likewise to be confined. 'Tell me who they were and they shall get the same fate.' 'I dinna like to tell' said the boy. 'You must tell or I'll double your time.' 'Sandy Allison was there' 'Sandy Allison. What Sandy Allison?' 'Your ain Sandy Allison.' The Baillie was dumbfounded at last he said 'You may go home for this time; but if I catch you again you may depend on being punished'.

Outside the Beautiful Order, there was one family which deserves a special mention even though they never quite made their way into the inner circle—the Andersons, especially John and his son Thomas because something of the credit that has always been given to the Marshalls really should be

Thomas Anderson's. The father flourished in the mid-eighteenth century as a business partner of Provost William Stewart (probably in the leather trade, as the other two partners were glovers) and he married Catherine, daughter of Baillie Sandeman; who had been one of those unfortunate enough to be captured and held hostage by the Young Pretender's army in 1745. Tradition has it that this Anderson was a friend of Lord George Murray and, as such, was able to save the hostages from massacre in the Tolbooth. Anyway, his will showed that he died a rich man, owning property in South Street and in North (or High) Street, in Skinnergate, in Castle Gable, and adjoining St John's churchyard, all of which he left to his sons and his sons-in-law.

It is with one of these sons, Thomas Anderson, that we are now concerned—a merchant like his father, but also in the linen business, a partner with Provost Fechney, James Ramsay and others in a tack of the Town's Mills. More importantly, he embarked on property development, buying out his relatives, and also acquiring one half of the Blackfriars lands from John Richardson of Tullybelton and, later, the other half from Janet, widow of James Millar. It was on these lands that the 'New Town' was to be built—Rose Terrace, Atholl Street and Atholl Crescent. The idea for this has always been credited to Thomas Hay Marshall and, in the end, Marshall *did* do most of the development, but he cannot claim to have dreamed up the design. That was the work of this Thomas Anderson who, as far back as 1787 (when Marshall was still only a boy of 17) presented a memorial to the worthy magistrates of Perth and the Town Council that:

> He hath lately purchased from Mrs Miller her half of the Black-friars lands which, with his own half, he would wish to offer to the public for building on. And upon such a plan as might be perfectly agreeable to the town. For which purpose he would wish to bring all the grounds within the Regality.

There seems to have been no difficulty about the first stage but, before he could begin his 'principal street of good houses'—Rose Terrace—there was much else to be done. The course of the Balhousie lade had to be diverted and a new bridge built over it, and the holders of the tack of the snuff mill who used the lade had to be compensated; and the line of the road to Dunkeld had to be changed from running across

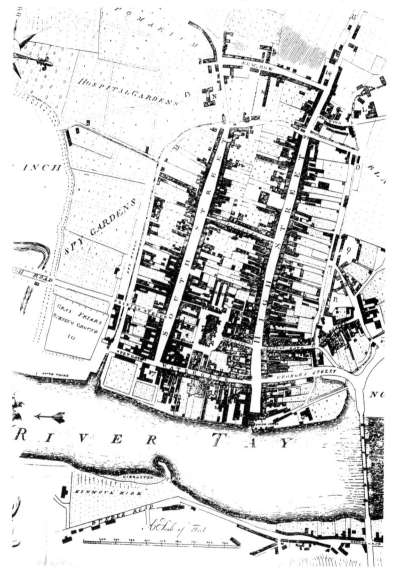

Plan of Perth, 1774, by Rutherford (*Reproduced by permission of the National Library of Scotland*).

the North Inch to the line that it follows today. All of this was accomplished in the early 1790s, most of it by 1792. That Anderson's plan went much further is shown by a map made by MacFarlane in that year which marks (as planned) not only Rose Terrace but also the streets which we now know as Barossa Street, Stormont Street and Melville Street, i.e. the town's boundaries.

MacFarlane shows the whole area quite clearly as the property of Anderson, and there is further confirmation in

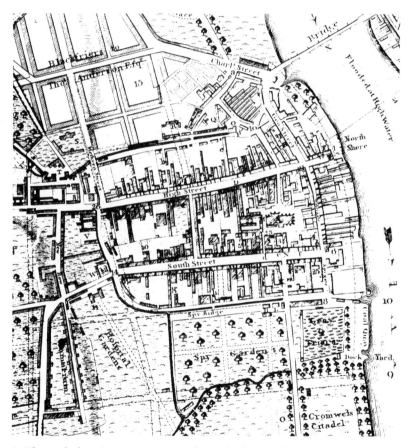

A Plan of the Ancient Town of Perth, by William Macfarlane, 4 June 1792 (*Reproduced by permission of Perth and Kinross District Council Museums and Art Galleries Department, Scotland*).

Robert Heron's *Observations made on a Journey through the Western Counties of Scotland, 1793* in which he states that Thomas Anderson had 'recently proposed a New Town to be built at a small distance west from Charlotte Street'. And it was Anderson who laid down in 1795 the conditions under which Rose Terrace was to be built. There were to be thirteen lots; each purchaser was to build, within two years, a house of stone with ashlar front, and roof of blue slate, of the same colour as that of the three houses already erected; the houses to consist of a vault and a ground floor with two other storeys and garrets above. Each householder would have 112 feet of land behind his house which was not to be used for the making of soap or candles, glass or vitriol, nor for boiling yarn, slaughtering or coppersmithing, nor for a 'Chymistry's Laboratory', nor for any other purpose which might give offence to neighbours. And each was to lay paving stones in front of his house, and to make, and keep, a grass bank sloping down to the then open lade, that ran between the terrace and the North Inch.

Incidentally, it is also to Anderson that we owe the continued existence of the extensive view over the North Inch from Atholl Street. He laid it down as a condition that no further houses should be built on the north side of Charlotte Street, in return for his having given more land *to* the Town than he received *from* it during the process of realigning the lade.

Even as late as 1799, a letter preserved in the Town's records declares: 'that he has some and intends to build *more*, houses facing the North Inch, and undertakes to use an architect agreeable to the town'. By that year he was, in fact, financially embarrassed, but such had not been the case when, seven years earlier, he was a considerable landowner and had special status as one of the few merchants in the town who was a heritor. Everyone regarded him as a man of substance, and his daughter Rose as an heiress—an eminently suitable bride for the up-and-coming son of another wealthy merchant. Sure enough, in that year 1792, Rose Anderson was married (with the promise of a tocher of £3,000) to Thomas Hay Marshall. Who was this fortunate young man?

He was as we have seen, the eldest surviving son of an older Thomas Marshall who was very much a member of the 'Beautiful Order'. When he was the Town's Treasurer in the early 1760s the father had been closely concerned in the founding of the new Perth Academy; and when Provost in the years 1784–6, with the paving of the Watergate and the High Street, and the planning of the first houses in Charlotte Street. He had a shop in the High Street 'below the Skinnergate' and imported (in partnership with Patrick Stewart) pearl-ash from Riga and (on his own) linseed and flax from Rotterdam. Another business partner was James Duncan (very likely his wife's brother) with whom he shared, at one time, a tack of the Inchyra fishings and of the snuff mill. He was also a pioneer in the adaptation of water power to the manufacture of linen, being a founder member of the New Row Company; as such, he was one of the merchants who signed a memorial to the noblemen and gentlemen of the county, sitting in Quarter Sessions in 1772, which is still preserved in the Perth Museum; it bemoans the decline of the local linen industry and asks for support in opposing foreign imports. He was, with Thomas Anderson, a founder director of the Perth Banking Company of 1787 and its first preses. Not surprisingly, Thomas Marshall had married, within the inner circle, a lady called Isabella Duncan who provided him, in due course, with seven daughters and four sons (See Appendix A). Fortunately his business concerns were sufficiently prosperous for him to be able to provide for those who survived, and his heirs were able, at his death, to recover considerable sums from the New Row Company, and also £4,500 that he had lent to the town.

Of his seven daughters, who were all born before 1766 and all still alive in that year, we know little except for Ann who married the Sheriff Clerk, James Patton; of the sons, James Marshall the eldest son died before his father, leaving his brother William as potential head of the family. As such, William was set up in his father's linen concern and also (along with James Patton, William Sandeman and the famous Richard Arkwright) in the new cotton mill at Stanley; and, even before his father died, William had succeeded to the

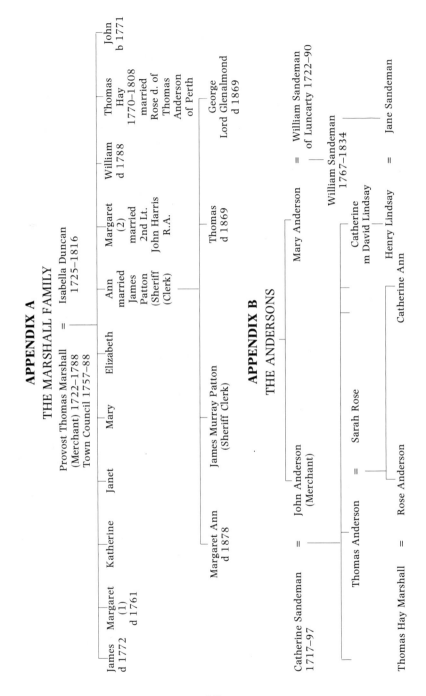

APPENDIX A

THE MARSHALL FAMILY

Provost Thomas Marshall 1722–1788 = Isabella Duncan
(Merchant) 1725–1816
Town Council 1757–88

James | Margaret | Katherine | Janet | Mary | Elizabeth | Ann | Margaret | William | Thomas | John
d 1772 | (1) | | | | | married | (2) | d 1788 | Hay | b 1771
d 1761					James	married		1770–1808
					Patton	2nd Lt.		married
					(Sheriff	John Harris		Rose d. of
					(Clerk)	R.A.		Thomas
								Anderson
								of Perth

James Murray Patton
(Sheriff Clerk)

Thomas
d 1869

George
Lord Glenalmond
d 1869

Margaret Ann
d 1878

APPENDIX B

THE ANDERSONS

Catherine Sandeman = John Anderson   Mary Anderson = William Sandeman
1717–97   (Merchant)   of Luncarty 1722–90

Thomas Anderson = Sarah Rose   William Sandeman
                                      1767–1834

                    Catherine
                    m David Lindsay

Thomas Hay Marshall = Rose Anderson   Henry Lindsay = Jane Sandeman

Catherine Ann

family place on the Town Council. But not for long. He died in the same year as his father, in 1788, so that the third brother had to take over at 18—Thomas Hay Marshall, Notwithstanding his youth, Thomas Hay not only became a partner in both his father's and his brother's businesses but, within two years had embarked on a venture of his own—and had stepped into their shoes as a member of the Town Council.

In 1790 he laid before it a memorial that:

> whereas he is informed that the lease of the wauk mills is now expired and, having in agitation to erect certain machinery for the purpose of carrying on a manufacture which will probably be of advantage to the town, and considering that these mills would suit the purpose intended, he humbly requests that the lease of these mills be set to public roup. And that the present holders of them be in no way incommoded, he humbly suggests that, as there is at present vacant, a fall which was formerly used for an old oil mill, which fall, though unfit for his purposes, he is informed would answer the purposes of a wauk mill in all respects equal with the present . . .

The application was successful and may have been the start of a firm trading as Stewart and Black, in which the ubiquitous Patrick Stewart and James Patton were also partners. From this, he followed his father into the Perth Banking Company and, like him, became its preses. And, by 1795, he had moved into property development, building 'the crescent fronting the Crieff Road' which we know as Atholl Crescent. He wrote to the Council:

> Sirs,   5 Nov 1796
> Having been at considerable expense in making a footpath along the Crieff Road and putting up lamp posts to where it joins the town's property; and as the footpath has been further extended as far as the Barracks and makes one of the most agreeable walks for the inhabitants, particularly in bad weather, it now wants nothing but the town's stepping in and finishing the small part of it which lies between the end of Charlotte Street and the town's lade of Balhousie. . . .

He had also built (or Anderson had) the mansion at the southern corner of Rose Terrace which has always been known to have been his 'house', though there is doubt as to whether he ever actually lived in it. And he was about to buy out his father-in-law to become the owner of all the

Provost T. H. Marshall's house at the corner of Rose Terrace.

Blackfriars lands and to take over as the principal developer of Rose Terrace. As such he donated the site for the new building to house the Academy and the Grammar School in January, 1802.

This might seem enough to occupy the energies of a young man still in his twenties, but he also was throwing himself into civic life with equal enthusiasm. In 1791, he, like his father, became the Town's Treasurer, and a Merchant Bailie in the following year, aged only 22. As such, he took the initiative in approaching the Earl of Kinnoull to secure the excambion of lands which doubled the size of the North Inch, to benefit the inhabitants of Perth and to provide a race-course. And, when the War Office approached the town to secure some land on which they could build a barracks to house three troops of dragoons, the Council put Thomas Hay Marshall in charge of the negotiations which led to the army acquiring the then wooded area of Drumhar. By 1800 he was Provost and, during the bad winter of 1801/2, was active in trying to relieve distress for the many families near to starvation. 'It was not uncommon', wrote Penny, 'to see the Lord Provost or a reverend gentleman standing over the boiler and handing out broth in John Street with a queue up as far as

Meal Vennel; and, with the soup, each got a small loaf at reduced price'. He is also credited with having arranged the excambions on the South Inch necessary for the building of Marshall Place, and with masterminding the feuing out of the Burghmuir. In his time, St John Street was opened up, and the dilapidated Gowrie House acquired by the town, and expansion continued to the west. But even all this did not exhaust Marshall's energies, for he also threw himself into amateur soldiering. Scotland had been denuded in the 1790s of the regular troops on which, in the absence of a proper police force, the authorities had to rely to keep the peace in any emergency—especially in towns such as Perth with its strong radical element. Regiments of Volunteers were raised, and when, in 1794, Provost Ramsay offered to provide three companies of thirty-eight men each, we find Marshall and his brother-in-law James Paton as Captains commanding two of them. They were to parade for drill for three hours twice a week and, if they did so, were to be paid. The men's uniforms eventually decided on—red jackets with blue facings and white breeks—had to be provided by the officers. Recruiting may have been helped by the fact that the drills seem to have been somewhat convivial occasions with a good deal of tippling beforehand, and the wives complaining that their men did not come home when the parades were over but hung about in the town's taverns. Whether for this reason, or because those who joined were exempted from the hated Militia with its wider commitments further afield, there was no difficulty in raising a second battalion of Volunteers when the situation abroad deteriorated in 1797. This time there were four companies of fifty men each, and a regimental band which grew from a diminutive four fifes and drums to a considerable body trained by an émigré French Count—13 fifes and drums and 12 further musicians with unspecified instruments. Provost Fechney took nominal command of this 2nd battalion in view of his civic position but he was elderly and corpulent and wholly ignorant of military tactics, and it is clear that it was Marshall, by now a major and second in command, who was the effective power behind the scenes.

When the question of pay arose, it was Marshall, not Fechney, who wrote to the Duke of Atholl, the Lord Lieutenant:

Perth 1 Sep 1797

My Lord Duke

In consequence of the present ferment (the militia riots) most of the cavalry stationed here have been ordered to different parts of the country. Colonel Rock and Provost Fechney have therefore ordered the 1st and 2nd Bns of Volunteers to mount guard and do duty in Town alternatively, of which step I have no doubt Your Grace will approve. Being thus on guard or at drill, with a view to bringing them forward speedily, the men conceive that they are out on actual service and are entitled to full pay in terms of the Volunteer Act. But upon this subject we should wish to be honoured with Your Grace's opinion. I have the honour to be

My Lord Duke, your Grace's humble servant

Tho Hay Marshall

Major 2nd Royal Perth Volunteers

And it was Marshall who reported, in another letter to the Duke, that the marching of his new corps was up to standard and that they wished to perfect their drill before leaving for the harvest. He enquires whether the Duke had been able to get him the assistance for which he had asked, or whether he had better seek help from the artillery in Perth or from recruiting parties there.

This was the time when the authorities were trying to compile lists of all the able-bodied young men who were not exempt and could be balloted for compulsory service with the hated Militia. In the country districts the unfortunate school-masters who had to draw up the lists came under much intimidation while, in Perth itself, the duty fell on the consta-bles who 'resolutely and consistently refused to do so. . . . because they deem their lives and property are in danger'. When the riots that broke out at Weem looked like spreading to Blair Atholl, Colonel Rooke (as he was more properly spelled) sent a party of his Windsor Foresters (cavalry) accom-panied by 40 men from Auchtergaven to apprehend the leaders of the rioters. These 40 Volunteers had not yet been embodied and Rooke had to borrow weapons for them—which he did—(once more) from Marshall, as Mr Stobie, the Duke's factor, reported to him:

8 Sept

My Lord Duke

Captain Stewart and I went to Perth and got from Colonel Rooke 40 stand of arms . . . With these we marched from the barracks to Mrs Marshall's to take refreshment and thence up the whole line of the High Street to the Toll with the Perth Volunteers Band playing before us.

According to Penny, a leader of the Radicals, the Volunteers were 'frequently' called upon to quell riots. During the early part of the war, the price of grain was often very high, sometimes owing to bad harvests, and sometimes to obstructions in the communications between the different parts of the country, and the impediments which the war threw in the way of commerce. The first occasion on which the Volunteers were called into service arose out of the following trifling circumstances. A gentleman of rather timid character, who was a speculator in grain, and a dealer in yarn and other commodities, inquired one day at a manufacturer with whom he had been transacting business, what the weavers were saying about the scarcity of meal—to which it was jocularly replied that they were threatening to have a riot to turn out the grain which they conceived the dealers had in store. This information threw the grain dealer into the utmost consternation. He instantly repaired to the magistrates, and succeeded in imparting to them a portion of the fear which distracted himself; the result of which was an order for a Captain's guard of forty men to meet in the Council Room that night. This intelligence soon spread to the west end of the town; and the general belief of the weavers being that the Volunteers would never stand opposition, a row was of course determined on, that they might have an opportunity of at once and for ever putting them down. The guard had assembled, and were making themselves extremely comfortable over the good things that had been provided for them, when information was received that a large body of people were on their way to the Magdalens, then tenanted by Mr Laurence

Buchan. A party of twenty men was dispatched, under the command of Captain Archer. Taking a near cut through the Inch, they pushed on with all haste—but, as many of the corps were more distinguished for rotundity than for speed of foot, these were sadly distressed by the time the hill was ascended. They arrived at last when the work of destruction was at its height—Mr Buchan had been considerably hurt in endeavouring to defend his property, and his wife and daughter had retired to the garret; the windows were demolishing, and the furniture was beginning to share the same fate. Upon the appearance of 'The White Feathers', however, the whole decamped with such precipitation that only one individual, a wright boy, who appeared to have been a mere spectator, was seized near Craigie Bridge, in the retreat, the Perth burghers being traditionally celebrated for their success in accomplishing the retrograde movement. One individual who was remarkable for boasting of his courage was seized with such a panic that he never looked behind until he reached the woods of Dupplin, where he lay concealed for some days, until the pangs of hunger forced him to venture back into the town. On their return from Mr Buchan's, the Volunteers were somewhat roughly handled by the democrats on their way down Leonard Street, where piles of stones had been prepared for the purpose; however by their firmness and forbearance, no serious accident occurred. Not long after this, the Volunteers were again said to have been called out to disperse a crowd that was trying to unload a ship that was to export grain from the neighbourhood. They had loaded their weapons with ball cartridge but fortunately were not called on to discharge them owing to the influence of Provost Caw in restraining the crowd. There is no evidence that Marshall (by now a Major) was personally concerned on either occasion but he and his superior, Lt Col Sharp of Kincarrathie (formerly of the 70th Regiment), received the thanks of the authorities on Oct 3 1797 at a meeting of the Highways Commissioners 'for their judicious and active assistance in maintaining order'.

I have searched in vain for any other instance to confirm Penny's claim that they were often called out, though the

Coupar Angus Company were called to Meigle, and, as we have seen, the Auchtergaven Volunteers marched with the Windsor Foresters to Blair, in the same year.

Somehow or another, Provost Lt Col Fechney managed to survive an inspection in March 1799, but when a Regular Officer called on him to exercise his regiment on the North Inch in 1801, he protested his inability and resigned in favour of Marshall. In fact, this was followed by a brief interlude of peace and the Volunteers were stood down, probably to their relief, though not as much so as in the case of the Militia, of whom Penny reported that 'on April 30 1802 there never was such a day in Perth. The privates got all the post chaises they could muster, filled them with the officers, after drawing them to the North Inch, where they were disembodied, took them back to the town in the same style, and carried them from their carriage to the Inn on their shoulders . . .' No doubt Marshall, who was by now Provost, was present.

In fact, the respite was short and in the following year the Perth Volunteers were reconstituted, this time as just one Battalion under Lt Col T.H. Marshall's command. An inspection in January 1804 reported that they had already been embodied and done duty for twenty one days, and were fit to serve alongside Regular troops, and to take any duty that might be required. Their officers were willing and capable. Similar reports were earned in 1805/6 until a scrimping government in London laid down that, in future, any new recruits would receive no allowances for clothing and no pay. Nor would the unit in future receive assistance in training from experienced drill-sergeants. The officers immediately resigned in a body, pointing out that these new regulations were tantamount to a 'dissolution of their corps; for as it is chiefly composed of tradesmen, who owing to a change in residence, or an occasional increase in employment, are continually withdrawn from it, we can have no hope that their places will be supplied if others are not tempted to offer their services by any compensation of their time, and must naturally be deterred by the mortifying distinction between the old and the newly established. . . .'

This was probably no surprise to the Duke of Atholl, the Lord Lieutenant, as, earlier in the year, he himself had listed a number of reasons why the new regulations should not be introduced. Nor do the local gentry seem to have disapproved because, when they met for the September Quarter Sessions, no less a distinguished figure than Colonel Graham, later Lord Lynedoch, proposed a motion which was carried, thanking the Volunteers for their services, and agreeing that there was little hope that they could continue in the existing circumstances, thus doing away with a body of men 'fully adequate to act with our Regular troops'.

The officers who had never taken their pay for themselves but had put it into a contingency fund decided that it should be devoted to the building of the new Academy. Marshall was empowered to hand over more than £1,000.

CHAPTER FIVE

A Sad Story

Sadly, Marshall, whose public life had been crowned with success, had not been so happy in his marriage, though, according to his own account, 'he flattered himself that, for the first three years, he had secured a considerable measure of that domestic comfort and happiness. . . . which may be the principal, if not the only, object in entering into a matrimonial connection. If he had to tax his wife with any fault, he might, with justice, have observed that in her personal expenses she was somewhat profuse'.

During these years, the couple had lived on the first floor of one of the new houses on the north side of Charlotte Street, above Andrew Gray (whose shop was on the street level) while the upper storey was rented by the Rev. Mr. Moodie whose servants kept chickens in the basement. All this emerges from a petition to the Consistory Court when Marshall sought a divorce on the grounds of his wife's adultery. The petition continues: 'subsequently to the period now alluded to, he had occasion to be sometimes away from home, having been called to London, Edinburgh and elsewhere in prosecution of his business, and although his absence on such occasions never exceeded a few weeks at a time, he afterwards found unfortunately that she availed herself of such opportunities to form connections with other men . . . irreconcilable to the solemn vows she had undertaken', and so, on 25 May 1796 he instituted a process of divorce, naming in the process, two officers who had been stationed in Perth during 1795—the Earl of Elgin (of Elgin Marbles fame) who was commanding his own regiment of Fencibles, and a Dr Harrison, Medical Officer to the Durham Rangers.

The Earl of Elgin had been staying in lodgings in Charlotte Street, just across the road, and a number of servants were called to show that, when Hay Marshall was away from home,

Portrait of Thomas Hay Marshall, Provost of Perth, 1800–01 and 1804–05, by David Junor. Oil on canvas, *c.* 1800 (*Reproduced by permission of Perth and Kinross District Council Museums and Art Galleries Department, Scotland*).

Rose and he exchanged signals from their windows and sent each other frequent notes; that they constantly walked about Perth arm-in-arm; that he visited her late at night when they sat together in the gloaming, refused to have candles brought, and even blocked up the keyhole so that they should not be watched; and, finally, that they went for a walk together up Kinnoull Hill (which was said to have a bad reputation) and disappeared into a thicket there.

The Earl soon departed, but much the same sort of allegations were made against Dr Harrison with the addition that, in his case, there was evidence that Rose had given him a ring and some lace handkerchiefs which she had had specially embroidered. And two letters of hers were intercepted in which she proclaimed her affection for him and her distress that he was about to leave Perth.

Rose's answer was to admit most of the facts but to deny that adultery had occurred. She claimed that her marriage had been unhappy from the start; that she had been forced into it by her parents; that Marshall had no interest other than a substantial tocher and the reversion of her father's estate when he died; that he had kept open house for all officers stationed in Perth and so had been responsible for contributing to, and therefore excusing, any improprieties of which she might have been guilty. Her final thrust was to allege that Hay Marshall had never shown any signs of displeasure with her until

> an event occurred which seems to have been the immediate cause of his bringing the present process. The circumstances of the defendant's father had always been considered in a most flourishing state till the beginning of the year 1796. At that time an embarrassment took place, when a few of his friends and, among others, his son-in-law, were called upon to look into them, when, to his astonishment . . . he found that (contrary to his expectations) his father-in-law's estate was indeed bankrupt, and that he must rank as a creditor for even the £3000 as the defendant's tocher . . . and that within a fortnight or three weeks she was served with a summons of divorce; that she was turned out of the house and only allowed £100 a year when she went to live with her parents, until prevented by the sneer of a country town from even appearing in the street with comfort she was obliged to move to Edinburgh, and afterwards, for the same reason, to London.

In London she ran up debts in his name. In later suits about these debts (1802) she claimed that

> he is a very considerable merchant in Perth and the first magistrate of the town. He is besides proprietor of some very valuable property called the Blackfriars in the immediate neighbourhood of Perth, on which a new town is daily building, and the property of several houses, one of which belongs to himself . . . estimated at £5000. And he has also drawn a dividend from the estate of the petitioner's father

to the amount of upwards of £1000 . . . yet he was not even paying the £100 a year due to her.

His answer to this suit was that

his income is not such as to enable him to pay even the £100. . . . The fact is that his income consisted almost entirely in the manufacture of linen and cotton cloths which has for the last two or three years been attended with loss. He has further suffered considerably by a concern in a cotton mill at Stanley. . . . He has been rather unsuccessful also in the speculation of building houses adjacent to the North Inch; and his situation is on the whole such that his present free income is scarce £200 per annum.

As to the rights and wrongs of the divorce allegations and of the subsequent financial wranglings, we cannot be sure, nor as to some allegations that Hay Marshall had himself been guilty of misconduct with two named prostitutes of Perth. The Commissary Court refused to accept this last. But they also refused to draw the inference that Marshall wanted as to Rose's adultery. My own impression is that Rose probably had been unfaithful. Certainly she had been wildly indiscreet and her own parents had been clearly disturbed by her behaviour—so much so that, on the day of the notorious walk on Kinnoull Hill, they had followed her and, when they found the climb too steep, had sat in the wood-keeper's cottage and paid the wood-keeper's nineteen-year-old son to search for the couple. And, on another occasion, after an evening party, Rose's mother had found the Earl with her; he had promised to return immediately to his lodgings but, as soon as the old lady's back was turned, he was once more with Rose. And it was pretty damning too that Rose had (in Marshall's absence in London) arranged for a settee, a grate for a fire, some chairs, silver spoons and wine glasses and sweetmeats to be transferred from the Charlotte Street lodging to the new but as yet unfurnished mansion in Rose Terrace, so that she could entertain her admirers under less close scrutiny than in the narrow Charlotte Street; especially as all this furniture was hurriedly retrieved when Marshall announced his impending return. And in the case of the doctor she admitted that she loved him better than her husband and that she had allowed 'a feeling towards him to develop which she ought to have repressed'. And she admitted bribing the servants to carry her letters and her gifts to him and to keep their mouths shut (which they did not).

Be that as it may, she departed first for Edinburgh, then, for a time, to Yorkshire (under whose protection we do not know) but she certainly met Lord Elgin there on one occasion, possibly to concert evidence, and then for London. While in Yorkshire she engaged a servant whose wages she failed to pay, and from whom she borrowed the money she needed in order to go to London. Here she went shopping in Bond Street, then, as now, not the least expensive neighbourhood. Bills survive in the Sandeman Library which show that, in the spring of 1799, she bought a 'lady's habit of superfine dark blue cloth with two rows of double gilt buttons', and a similar one of brown cloth with three rows of gold buttons, two silk corsets and two velvet collars, two coloured bonnets and two livery round hats, together with three more hats later in the year and a fur cape. Hay Marshall had paid some of her earlier bills, but he drew the line at this one as he had issued an inhibition two years before.

By 1800 she was back with her parents who by then had moved to Edinburgh, either through embarrassment at the prolonged divorce proceedings, or, more likely, to avoid Anderson's creditors. And, of course, just as there were officers in Perth, so there were officers in and around Edinburgh—and Rose had not changed. This time there was incontrovertible evidence that she had been seen actually in bed with an officer who was lodging in her father's house—a John Cooper Esquire, also of the Durham Militia; and that she had taken lodgings in Leith so as to be nearer to Lieutenant Edgar of the Royal Artillery at the fort or battery between Newhaven and Leith; and that after one of her late-night visits to the latter, her corsets and various other articles had to be returned to her the following morning. So, in December 1803, the Provost (for so he now was) renewed his proceedings and at last got his divorce.

Letters were still being addressed to him in Charlotte Street in 1798, two years after the separation. And we know that he did not marry again, and that when he died in 1808 it was at Bowerswell on Kinnoull Hill, so it is unlikely that he ever actually moved into the Rose Terrace mansion. It would have been inconveniently large for one man living alone, used as he was to the cramped accommodation in Charlotte Street.

He may have let it, or even sold it, since it is not specifically mentioned in his will, though another house is—Whistlecroft, across the river; which stood where the Norie Miller Gardens now are. According to Penny, he had just finished building it and was about to move in, when he died. James Patton rechristened it Marshall Lodge.

Marshall must have been lonely at the end, and anxious about money matters, but he should, at least, have been comfortable, with two servants to look after him and a well-equipped household. For his living rooms he had 18 bamboo chairs (just beginning to be fashionable), a square mahogany table, four hall chairs, a writing desk, a bureau bookcase and bookstand, a backgammon table, a mahogany knife box, a clock and case, a chest of drawers and a fender with fire irons. Upstairs there was a bed and bedstead and two feather beds, a hair mattress and a straw one. His second chest of drawers, his basin stand and night table, were all of mahogany, and there were ample sheets, pillow-slips and blankets. And there was a generous provision of table-silver, china and glass as befitted the entertaining which a Provost must have had to do. But it was his cellars which were really lavishly supplied. He cannot have had any premonition of an early death or he would scarcely have laid down two pipes (184 gallons) of old port, 110 dozen bottles of good port, 21 dozen of thin port and 23 dozen of thin dreg port—to say nothing of 14 dozen of sherry, 22 dozen of claret and 18 dozen of madeira. His cellars must themselves have been large, as they contained in addition no fewer than three gross of empty bottles when the inventory came to be taken. For adornment, he sported a gold chain and a watch by Pinchbeck, a pair of pistols, four swords and a dirk. Curiously, the only picture mentioned was one hanging in his warehouse, and there is no mention of the portrait of him which is now in the Perth Museum and Art Gallery. One would suppose that it would have belonged to him, unless, of course, it was painted posthumously.

The divorce brought little relief; indeed, the last three years of Marshall's life were amongst the busiest and most anxious, as may be seen from two letters to the Duke of Atholl's agent, Mr Palliser. Not only had he had the worry of the Volunteers but he also did a second spell as Provost from 1804–6; and he was trying to serve the Duke in a variety of ways—over Parliamentary elections, and as go-between in the Duke's need to raise £40,000 urgently by selling off outlying parts of his estates. He failed to find enough willing buyers to achieve this last, though he himself managed to buy the Glenalmond division with the aid of his brother-in-law. But he did succeed in swinging the Town's support behind Sir David Wedderburn, the Duke's candidate for the next Parliamentary election. The Council had been approached in March 1806 by Sir David and also by a Major Ramsay who was backed by the Earl of Breadalbane; Ramsay had eight supporters on the Council to Wedderburn's twelve. But, by the time that Marshall had 'got the bowls to roll the right way' six months later, Wedderburn received unanimous support. The Mr Rutherford referred to below was a Perth lawyer, acting on behalf of Major Ramsay.

To Mr Palliser, Dunkeld House   Perth 24 Sep 1806
My dear Sir

I had the pleasure to receive your esteemed of 21 and also the haunch of venison which His Grace was so good as to send. I presented it to Sir David Wedderburn who gave us the dinner yesterday and told Sir David that His Grace had sent it for that purpose. He had brought up one from Ballindean . . . but took it back again. The Devil such a week as I had, ever since I came into the Town Council, but, thanks be praised, I have got the bowles to roll the right way. Lord Breadalbane has been keeping open house all this week and giving claret at the mart where red-nosed Fraser is his representative, and a pretty one he makes. Between ourselves, John Rutherford has given a great deal of trouble. I would despise to take notice of it but to you in confidence and I beg may go no farther.

A hint—if His Grace means to send any venison on Monday (presumably for a dinner in connection with the 'elections' to the Town Council) please say that instead of one, he would be pleased to send two, as every individual must have a piece, and I have been horribly puzzled to divide it into 80 or 90 bits. If you can do this in the most delicate way, I will be obliged. . . .

And to the same he wrote, two years later:

29 April 1808

. . . I had a letter from His Grace last night agreeing to an offer I made of £12,000 (for Glenalmond) . . . I must stir myself to procure the needful from some of my friends—I think Mr Paton may be able to assist me. I feel much better than when I had the pleasure of seeing you, and you may suppose that it will add much to my pleasure to see you again now that I can have the satisfaction to converse with you without pain. The Duke's friendly letter has done me more good than all the Doctor's stuff put together. . . .

As can be seen, Marshall was by now a sick man, and this is confirmed in the correspondence of his own man of business, Mr Peddie, the Town Clerk, to whom a friend wrote in the same month, 'I was extremely sorry to hear that Mr Marshall was complaining. If he were to be taken off, the town of Perth would suffer an irreparable loss. . . .' But he kept at work and attended a Town Council meeting on June 6th and, on June 24, wrote to Peddie:

My Dear Sir, A sight of you would do me good. I really wish you would come over and give me the news.

T.H. Marshall

and a week later, still in a firm hand:

July 1st 1808

Old Farquhar has drawn upon me for two years rents of Huntingtower for which he says I am liable. Now, as you have the charter, I beg you will send it by the bearer that I may be certain—as I think—that he is wrong. I wish to see the book where the Blackfriars feus are, which I will return in a day or two, as I understand Hepburn wishes to deviate from the elevation of the end house in the Terrace.*

Believe me, my dear Sir

Thomas Hay Marshall.

---

*Hepburn *did* do so. The house at the north end of Rose Terrace does not match Marshall's house at the south end.

He died just a fortnight later—of 'water in the chest'—having retained his ability to jest, up to the end, concluding another letter to Mr Palliser, '. . . This is a very good prospect of a man going to *** and who, ten thousand chances to one will never reap a farthing of it (his purchase of Glenalmond). When Bishop Niven preaches upon Death, you may give him the above for a text'.

All Marshall's estate was bequeathed to his brother-in-law, James Patton, on condition that he paid annuities to Marshall's mother and to his only surviving brother John (with a stipulation that none of it was to go to pay off John's debts) and to two servants, John Reid and Betty Wilson. With it went the lands of Glenalmond; those parts of the Blackfriars lands that he had bought from Thomas Anderson and from Anderson's trustee in bankruptcy, the unrelated Willam Marshall; his father's lands on the north side of the High Street, and the large stock of goods in his linen and cotton manufactory (valued at £1,900) and the new house on the east side of the Tay, later known as Marshall Lodge when lived in by Patton. It should have been a magnificent inheritance but, when the final reckoning was done, there was still over £12,000 owing to the Duke, and another £10,000 to other creditors, while the debts owing *to* him, together with other goods, were only worth £9,391. Patton had to declare this deficiency but somehow managed to hold on to Glenalmond which he was thus able to add to the adjoining estate of the Cairneys which he had bought from Col. Graham.

Just how much Marshall had achieved may be seen by looking at three town plans, the dates of which happen almost to coincide with his birth, his entry into public life, and his death. Rutherford's map of 1774 shows how Perth at that time was still virtually confined to the limits of the mediaeval city walls, with just a few houses overspilling to the north and west. The one major development was Smeaton's new bridge over the Tay, and George Street giving access to it. The Academy has been started but is still housed above a former granary at the foot of St John's Kirk. There is as yet no St John Street.

Even MacFarlane's plan of 1792 shows little new building

except for a few houses in Charlotte Street, though there had been some progress that would not show on a map, such as the lighting and paving of the more important thoroughfares. And the free passage of traffic has been further facilitated by the breaching of the town walls, the widening of the ports and the removal of the Cross. The really significant feature of the map is that it shows the future developments that were as yet only in the planning stage; the new turnpike road to Dunkeld, to take the place of that running across the North Inch; a New Town bounded roughly by what is now Barossa Place, Barrack Street, Atholl Street and Rose Terrace, together with another New Town to the south, fronting the South Inch.

But by 1809 (Reid's plan in the Map Department of the National Library of Scotland) only seventeen years later, the great part of this has been accomplished with Marshall the driving force behind it all. Atholl Street, Atholl Crescent and Rose Terrace, with its fine central block to house both Academy and Grammar School; the Horse Barracks (later the Black Watch Depot); Canal Street, Mill Street and St John Street have all been completed; a start has been made on Marshall Place; and the size of the North Inch has been doubled.

So much for what he achieved in his short lifetime. But what sort of a person was he? Alas, that eludes us, since there are so few personal letters to help. His portrait suggests that he might have been rather a dull one; his statue a self-important one; Rose Anderson calls him mercenary; his will makes it clear that he may have been somewhat over-ambitious. But I am reluctant to accept these unflattering surmises. After all, tradition is against them, and so is the only obituary of him that can be taken seriously—that in the *Scots Magazine* for July 1808. The author, who must have known him personally, wrote that it was:

impossible to convey an adequate idea of the sorrow and regret universally produced in this place by the death of our late Chief Magistrate, Mr Marshall of Glenalmond . . . His remains were brought from his late residence, Bowerswell Lodge, attended by his relatives, together with the Duke of Atholl . . . The crowd which attended was immense, men, women and children pressing forward to witness the

Map of Perth by Reid, 1809 (*Reproduced by permission of the National Library of Scotland*).

final scenes . . . every warehouse and shop was shut . . . it is impossible to turn the eye to any quarter of this town or its environs without some remarkable remembrance of Provost Marshall coming into view. He had a particular pleasure in planning, and a particular energy in carrying out, whatever appealed to him as calculated to adorn, improve or in any way be beneficial to his native town.

That might have been enough, but the writer goes on to add a specific tribute to his personality:

As a private gentleman, he was no less respected and loved—affable, courteous and pleasing in his manners; he would be a barbarian indeed who would be at enmity with him.

CHAPTER SIX

A Walk Round Georgian Perth

We have seen how, for the first time, Perth had needed to expand and to pull down what remained of its crumbling mediaeval walls . . . George Street was the first important highway to be opened up—to give access to the new bridge. It was named after George III; Charlotte Street followed, named after his wife, and Atholl Place and Atholl Crescent and then Rose Terrace; this last was called after the surname of its initiator's wife. Later, on the southern edge, Marshall Place commemorates the Provost, with, leading to it, St John Street and Princes street. Tay Street opened up the riverside. It was fortunate that this major development should have taken place when fashions in architecture were so dignified. Too much of what was then built has since been destroyed or altered for the sake of shop fronts, but we still have an outer ring of Georgian building round the old city, and this has been designated a conservation area.

It may be explored in two walks, each starting from the same place at the river end of the High Street.

Our first proceeds northwards along George Street itself. One longs for the original frontages, but there is a gable over No. 23 which repays attention as does the rather later façade of the George Inn opened in 1775 and visited in 1845 by Queen Victoria and her family. Rough seas had prevented her return to London from Deeside by the royal yacht and the visit was unexpected. Cutlery and other conveniences had to be hurriedly borrowed, but so pleased was Her Majesty that she came again the following year and the inn has been the Royal George Hotel ever since. A modern extension to the rear gives a lovely view over the river. Across the road is Albert Close, presumably a new name for an ancient passage.

The Royal George Hotel.

Traditionally it claims the only surviving remnant of the old town walls, but it is doubtful whether there is any justification for this.

At the end of George street stands the Museum. When Thomas Hay Marshall died, it was widely felt that his services to the town ought to be marked by some memorial. Spurred on by the Duke of Atholl, a committee collected enough to build the Rotunda to the designs of David Morison of the printing family. Later the building was greatly increased in size by the Art Gallery added in 1935 as a result of a bequest from the late Robert Brough.

The Museum has received so many gifts over the years that it is not possible to display more than a fraction of its interesting material at any one time, and so the policy is to rotate what is on display. Hence any detailed description might be out of date as soon as it was written. But it is safe to say that, as in the past, there will always be something of interest for all ages and all tastes. Recently its natural history section has been entirely rearranged, with emphasis on the local environment, and there is also a new local history gallery of absorbing interest, containing among other things some of the most recent archaeological finds and also the last surviving costume of the Morris Dancers who performed for Charles I in 1603.

Upstairs around the foot of the dome are cases of communion tokens.

So far as the period with which this chapter is chiefly concerned there is some lovely Regency furniture, silver and glass—all crafts still practised with distinction in the city; and, of special interest, a case of ivory, bone and wooden items made by French prisoners of war, confined to prison in Perth during the Napoleonic Wars which they were allowed to sell to earn a little pocket money.

A great deal was recovered during the recent excavations and the Museum succeeded in its claim that such objects should be housed in Perth after full evaluation and the necessary conservation treatment. Among items already on show (in the Local History Gallery) are wooden combs and other articles of wood and horn for domestic use from the Middle Ages, and, even rarer because even more perishable, an ankle boot of soft leather and some fragments of textiles, including a silken hair net, imported from Germany.

Back in the main hall there is a bust of William Soutar by Benno Schotz, Sculptor-in-Ordinary to the Queen; paintings of Thomas Hay Marshall and of Dr Anderson, the many-talented Rector of the Academy; and a bust of Sir Walter Scott by Sir John Steell, with a relief below depicting Hal O' the Wynd and the Fair Maid of Perth.

The Art Gallery has a permanent collection which includes a wide variety of paintings, especially of those by Scottish Artists, and also provides a venue for other exhibitions such as the Annual Show of the Perth Arts Association.

Adjoining the Museum is a bow-fronted building, now a restaurant but once the Post Office, conveniently sited because it adjoined the alighting area for the stage coach. The

Smeaton's Bridge, opened 1771.

postmaster was George Sidey who, like his predecessor, Robert Morison, combined that office with printing and bookselling.

Smeaton's bridge was completed in 1771, at a cost of £20,631 12s 5¾d There had been earlier wooden bridges; one was washed away in 1210 and another had suffered the same fate in 1589, and a third in 1621, after which there was none for 150 years, but by this time traffic and trade had greatly increased and it was possible to raise a considerable part of the cost by public subscription, the list being headed by the Earl of Kinnoull—an interested party in that he owned the land at both ends of the bridge. This time Smeaton built so well that his work has stood the test of time and even proved strong enough to be widened in 1869 and to carry the town's trams until their demise in 1929. The house in Charlotte Street, next the bridge, is one of the most graceful and, unlike so many, has retained its original astragals—the wooden bars holding the window panes, and, also, above the door, the little brass sign of the company with which the owner had insured himself against fire, for, without that sign, the company's private fire brigade would render no aid.

Turning to the left, we pass a statue by William Brodie of the Prince Consort, unveiled by Queen Victoria in 1864 on one of her regular visits. She did not like eating while the royal train was in motion and Perth Station often happened to be a convenient stopping place.

Atholl Place and Atholl Crescent were designed by Sir Robert Reid, the architect of the lovely St George's Church in Charlotte Square, Edinburgh. The central house of the crescent has not only an attractive exterior but also a domed staircase within, ornamented with classical plaster work.

Reid was also the architect of Rose Terrace but in both cases the developer was Thomas Hay Marshall whose own intended dwelling was the one at the corner of the terrace with Atholl Street; given the domestic staff, it would have been a lovely one to live in with its big windows looking out over the North Inch and also south towards the sun. Central to his design was the new building for the Perth Academy with its Venetian windows, its pilasters and balustered skyline; only the statuary and the clock were later additions.

The Academy was founded to teach the modern subjects such as arithmetic, science and French (which the Grammar

The former Perth Academy in Rose Terrace.

83

School did not), the first of its sort in Scotland. A school is mentioned in the twelfth century at which time all education was in the hands of the church and a Grammar School (concentrating on Latin) in the sixteenth when its schoolmaster, Andrew Simon, was converted to the doctrines of the reformers by reading Sir David Lindsay's *Satire of the Three Estates*. When, in the mid-eighteenth century, the city fathers felt that a more utilitarian curriculum might be advantageous, T.H. Marshall's father was one of those who combined to found the Academy in 1760. From the first it taught literature, trigonometry, geometry, navigation, astronomy, geography and history, and it soon added chemistry, physics and French. It was for his son to organise the move from the original and unsuitable premises on the upper floors of the Corn Market (where the City Halls now stand in St John's Square) to Rose Terrace, where it remained until its removal to a splendid new site at Viewlands in 1932. At the time of writing, the old building is being converted into office accommodation now that the rest of the terrace has been refurbished, but Perth still waits with some trepidation to know the future of the large octagonal room which was the original teaching room for the Rector. It may have had poor acoustics but it was one of the town's architectural treasures.

Of the many distinguished Rectors the Academy has had, only the second to hold that office can be mentioned. Dr Adam Anderson ruled from 1809–37 and only left to become Professor of Natural Philosophy at St Andrews University. Most headmasters have to wait until they retire to receive tributes from their employers and their pupils but Anderson was so highly regarded that his pupils presented him with a silver cup at the end of his first year, and the Council increased his salary at the end of the second—and doubled it not long after—though it is true to say that this did not happen until he had pointed out that, so successful had the Academy been, that its methods were now being copied in a number of other Scottish cities and that the Rectors of their schools were being offered salaries considerably larger than his. Even more notable than his success as a teacher was his versatility and his public spirit, bringing both clean water and gaslighting to the town.

When the Academy building opened, the Grammar School moved there too, for nearly a hundred years. Now the name of the Grammar School belongs to the secondary school in North Muirton.

Further along Rose Terrace, a house bears a plaque stating that John Ruskin spent part of his boyhood there; he also contracted his disastrous marriage in Perth, across the river at Bowerswell.

At the end, a row of villas *c.* 1810–20 is named after the Peninsular War victory of Barossa, a triumph for one of Wellington's most trusted generals, Thomas Graham of Balgowan, later Lord Lynedoch. Another memorial—to him and to the regiment of Perthshire men that he raised—the 90th Perthshire Light Infantry—lies across the North Inch, near to the river. They were known as the Greybreeks from the colour of their uniform and were later linked to the Cameronians as their 2nd Battalion.

Perhaps even more widely appreciated than its Rose Terrace is Perth's North Inch. The near end had been an open space for grazing and for recreation as far back as memory went. Horse racing (transferred at the beginning of this century to more spacious ground at Scone Palace), football and golf go back at least as far as the sixteenth century—and tennis is recorded in the fifteenth—real or royal tennis that is, played in a walled court such as still exists at Falkland Palace.

As for football and golf, a quotation from the Kirk records states that

on Feb 21 1592 John Pitscottie . . . Finlay Errol . . . with several other persons were playing at football in the meadow inch of the Muirton . . . on the Sunday of the Fast, in the time of preaching in the forenoon . . . on Nov 19 1599 John Gardiner, James Bowman, Laurence Chalmers, and Laurence Cuthbert confessed that they were playing golf on the North Inch in the time of preaching afternoon on the Sabbath.

Both lots had, of course, to make public atonement. And it is known that there was a maker of golf clubs even earlier than that because he is referred to in the royal accounts during James IV's reign.

More organised golf dates from the foundation of the Royal Perth Golfing Society in 1824 and the King James VI Golf Club in 1858 (now with its separate course on Moncreiffe Island below the Queen's Bridge). One of its founders was a notorious character, the Rev. Charles Robertson ('Gowfing Charlie'), one of whose maxims was 'if ye're playing well, dinna taste. But, if ye're no playing well, ye may take a drappie'. The Perth Artisans' Club followed in 1866.

Football (and golf for the matter of that) came under fire not only from the Kirk but from successive Scottish Parliaments for fear that it might distract men from their patriotic duty to learn to shoot with bow and arrow. Football was also felt to be a 'bloody murderous pastime' until the drawing up of the Rugby Union and the Association Football codes in the second half of the nineteenth century. Just how fierce the game could be may be seen from an extract from the First Statistical Account of 1793:

> Every year on Shrove Tuesday, the bachelors and married men drew themselves up at the cross of Scone on opposite sides. A ball was thrown up, and they played from two o'clock till sunset. The game was this. He who at any time got the ball into his hands, ran with it till overtaken by one of the opposite party, and then, if he could shake himself free from those on the opposite side who seized him, ran on; if not, he threw the ball from him, unless it was wrested from him by the opposite party; but if no person, he was allowed to kick it. The object of the married men was to 'hang it' i.e. to put it three times into a small hole in the moor, the dool or limit on the one hand; that of the bachelors was to drown it, i.e. to dip it three times into a deep place in the river, the limit on the other. The party who could effect either of these objects won the day. But if neither party won, the ball was cut into equal halves at sunset. In the course of play one might always see some scene of violence between the parties; but, as the proverb of this part of the country has it, 'all was fair at the ball of Scone'.

and from an account (by J.D. Urquhart in his *Historical Sketches of Scone*) of a game played in the 1830s:

About fifty years ago Lord Stormont, the present Earl of Mansfield, arranged a football match on a large scale, with the Lord Provost of Perth, the players on each side to number fifty . . . The rendez-vous and battlefield was the North Inch of Perth, on which were assembled several hundreds of spectators to watch the grand match as it was very appropriately named. Mr Kemp, writer, led off for the Perth team, by kicking the ball up the Inch, where soon ensued a general melee. The ball getting into the river, one of the Scone team, James Loudfoot [? Proudfoot], ran in up to the armpits and brought it ashore, whereupon he was allowed the privilege of a free-kick. The game having continued for some time, with prospects of success for each side hanging in the balance, the bulk of the spectators, being inhabitants of Perth, crowded in past the goal and prevented the strangers from scoring, and also did everything in their power to assist the home team. At the end of the first hour, matters had assumed so serious an aspect that the game was abruptly stopped, and the strangers stoned off the pitch, some taking refuge in the offices of Mr Condie, North Port . . . Shortly after this, a challenge was sent by Lord Stormont to the Lord Provost to play forty-nine men a side, at any given place seven miles outside of Perth, when there might be a fair field and no favour, but the challenge was never accepted. Lord Stormont shortly afterwards entered into Parliament as the member for Perthshire and the game fell rapidly into disuse on his withdrawal from the post of Captain. When the custom continued, every man in the parish, the gentry not excepted, was obliged to turn out and support the side, and the person who declined to do his part on this occasion was fined.

When more uniform and more decorous rules were drawn up by the F.A. St Johnstone Football Club came into being in 1884–5 as an offshoot of a Cricket Club of the same name and (playing then in black and white) it gained its first victory over Hibernians in the following year. Blue and White was adopted in 1886. It attracted First Division status—and its ground at Muirton Park—in 1924. Highlights have been the semi-finals of the Cup in 1934 and 1991, and a great run in the 1960s with Henry Hall as its chief goal scorer.

Yet another benefit achieved in Thomas Hay Marshall's time was the doubling of the size of the North Inch by an exchange of land between the town and the Earl of Kinnoull who owned the northern end where the golf courses are.

Today, there is room for not only golf and football, but cricket and hockey and putting; boating from its banks, and fishing; swings for the children and seats for the elderly; and, of course, the whole range of indoor activities since the building of the magnificent Sports Centre by the Gannochy Trust.

The North Inch is particularly well planted with mature trees. Lovely all the year, though naturally at their best in spring and autumn, they seldom look tired even in the height of summer since their roots reach the high water table of what was once a flood plain. So too, the far bank of the river is well wooded and can be appreciated from the excellent path along the near side.

Another special feature for the tree-lover is a small garden next to the Sports Centre. This was laid out in 1962 as a memorial to the Victorian traveller and plant discoverer, David Douglas, son of a Scone stonemason. It is planted out with trees that he himself introduced from the Americas. Overlooking it is a beautifully sited home for the elderly, and also Balhousie Castle. The exterior that we see today is largely nineteenth century but it is pleasing and is built round a genuine sixteenth-century tower house. At one time the town residence of the Earls of Kinnoull, it now houses the head-quarters and Regimental museum of Perthshire's regiment, the Black Watch, open to the public and very well worth a visit. A pair of wrought-iron gates commemorates Field Marshal Earl Wavell, perhaps its most famous son. Her Majesty Queen Elizabeth the Queen Mother is the Colonel-in-Chief. As such, and also as the President of the Aberdeen Angus Society which has its Headquarters in Perth, she is a frequent visitor.

Further to the north is a line of villas which enjoy an uninterrupted view over the Inch to the river and the hills beyond but these are later in date and so we return to the middle of the town via Barossa Place, Melville Street with its large Roman Catholic church, and Kinnoull Street. This last has Pullars former factory and Gloags on the left, the Free Church, the Congregational Church and the Sandeman Library on the right. Gloags wine business was founded in 1814. The library was the result of a bequest from Professor

Balhousie Castle.

Archibald Sandeman, member of another family whose fortunes were based on the wine trade. This library is now part of the County Library services and houses upstairs a rich collection of books about the neighbourhood. Plans are afoot to move it to larger and more convenient premises in York Place.

An alternative route back would be by North Methven Street (1789) and the Episcopalian Cathedral of St Ninian. This was built in stages during the second half of the nineteenth century to the designs of William Butterfield, the architect of Keble College and of a number of other churches built in England during the Oxford Movement. The choir is the oldest part, then the nave and the Lady Chapel, the cloisters and the chapter house. It is large and sometimes dark and cold, but there is a deal of good workmanship to be admired and much has been done recently to lighten it. A rood screen was donated by Sir Francis Norie Miller (of General Accident) in memory of his elder son who lost his life when the troopship, *Transylvania*, was torpedoed in the Mediterranean on 4 May 1917.

Behind St Ninians, where there is now a housing development, there used to be a barracks, originally for cavalry, but later the depot of the Black Watch. Perth was a garrison town for two hundred years after the 1745—another factor possibly in her economic revival. The new development is best seen by passing through the wide arch labelled Drumhar Court to appreciate the effective restoration of the backs of the shops on the west side of North Methven Street.

To tour the other half of Georgian Perth, we start again at the foot of the High Street. This time we turn left up St John Street (1796–1801). As with George Street, the upper storeys are all that are left of the original buildings, though the somewhat later Bank of Scotland by David Rhind (1846) is substantial and well proportioned in what Osbert Lancaster would have called 'Banker's Renaissance'. To the left, Baxters Vennel and Oliphant's Vennel recall the city's connection with its bakers and with a neighbouring family (from Gask) famous for its fidelity to the Jacobite cause and for the songs written by Lady Nairne.

A. and G. Cairncross have recently changed hands, but for over a hundred years they were a family firm of jewellers from the days when the grandfather of the late owners owned a little shop, a photograph of which may be seen in the museum. They were justly renowned for the jewelry designed by the late Alastair Cairncross and for their connection with the pearl fisheries in the Tay and other home rivers, which go back beyond mediaeval days and were known to the Romans. They have on show the finest freshwater pearl found in recent times, perfectly formed and weighing 44½ grains, nicknamed after its finder, William Abernethy. At the end of St John Street, the Salutation Hotel provides a fitting backdrop.

A side step onwards and to your right leads into Princes Street and to the Greyfriars Burial ground which contains some of the country's most beautiful carved headstones; and then on, past St John's Episcopalian Church, to the South Inch, Perth's second wonderful open space for recreation. For two centuries it was somewhat marred by the Citadel, a great

Mariner's gravestone, Greyfriars Burial Ground (*Reproduced by permission of Betty Willsher and Doreen Hunter*).

Merchant's gravestone, Greyfriars Burial Ground (*Reproduced by permission of Betty Willsher and Doreen Hunter*).

earth and stone work put up by Cromwell, but this has long since been razed to the ground. Beyond it, far left, is Perth Prison.

At our backs is Marshall Place, the houses of which (mostly flats now) are compensated for not having quite such a lovely outlook as those on the North Inch by the fact that they face south and therefore get the sun and a wonderful display of crocuses in the spring. The Georgian terrace is only broken by the church of St Leonards-in-the-Fields, a successful essay in Gothic revival 1885.

To our right, at the western end of the Inch, is a row of detached villas of the same vintage, St Leonard's Bank, built

St Leonard's in the Fields in Marshall Place.

on land that was once the gardens of the King James VI Hospital. And, at the end of King Street, is a statue to Sir Walter Scott. It was bought by the city fathers in 1845 from the studio of the brothers Cochrane, local sculptors about to emigrate to America. First set up at the end of the High Street, it had to be moved, like the Mercat Cross, in order to facilitate the flow of traffic as it increased. He is in far quieter and more suitable surroundings here.

Turning towards the river, we reach another of Perth's interesting buildings—The Waterworks. As people became aware of the importance of hygiene and of an unpolluted water supply, Dr Anderson the versatile Rector of the Academy:

> originated the idea of supplying the city with water from Moncrieff Island; formed the plan for carrying it into effect; and superintended the execution of it. The water reservoir, which overlooks the Tay at the foot of Marshall Place, is one of the most admired architectural ornaments of Perth. Only a few days before his death he cyphered with chalk the inscription which the edifice now bears in cast iron

letters, *Aquam igne et aqua haurio* [I draw water by fire and water, i.e., steam].

So wrote one who was almost a contemporary of Rector Anderson. The water was pumped into a storage tank under the iron dome and the pillar attached to the Grecian temple served to conceal the necessary chimney. It is said, in the invaluable pamphlet, *Walks in Perth* by Mrs Elwena Fraser and Dr Margaret E.C. Stewart, that the scheme attracted the attention of the King of Prussia when it was completed in 1832 and that he asked that a facsimile of the design should be erected in Berlin. At any rate it sufficed to provide for the town's ever increasing needs until 1965 when new arrangements were made. Since then, the Perth Civic Trust, the Council and the Tourist Association skilfully converted it into

The Round House, built as the city's waterworks, now houses the Fergusson Collection.

a tourist centre where the visitor could get information about all the facilities in the area and help and guidance in planning his holiday. Unfortunately it was rather too remote and it has now been adapted to house a large collection of the paintings of J.D. Fergusson owned by the Fergusson Trust. The present tourist office is in the High Street, next to Skinnergate.

Nearby the railway bridge crosses the river on its way to Dundee with access also to Moncreiffe Island with its golf course and its allotments, while to our left is the Queen's Bridge (originally named after Queen Victoria). It was opened by Lady Pullar, wife of the Lord Provost in 1900, but it proved to be inadequate to carry the volume of traffic of the motor-car age. It had to be replaced with the present structure, which appropriately received a Royal opening in 1960, on the 750th anniversary of the granting of our Royal Charter by William the Lion.

Another development of the early 1800s was that of Tay Street. It is difficult to be fair to its principal feature, the County Buildings which contain the Sheriff Court and the County Hall. Sir Robert Smirke's Grecian Portico looks extremely well, especially from halfway across the bridge, but one cannot forget that, to put it there, it was necessary to pull down the old Gowrie House with all its historical associations, and also the Monks Tower erected by the Abbot of Lindores under pressure from the English King Edward III. The hall used to contain paintings by Lawrence of the 4th Duke of Atholl and General Lord Lynedoch, and also a Raeburn of Neil Gow, fiddler and composer.* Outside is a bronze panel depicting Gowrie House above, and the arms of the Earls of Gowrie and the Royal arms of Scotland.

Across South Street, we pass the Water Vennel—in former days the right-of-way for the humbler citizens down to the river, between the dwellings of the wealthy in the Watergate; then No. 44 Tay Street, the first home of General Accident; it now houses a display of items connected with the beginnings

---

*These are now in the care of the Museum and Art Gallery, but having suffered in the recent floods, they await restoration.

The County Buildings on Tay Street (*c.* 1820).

and the history of the Company; then the offices of the *Perthshire Advertiser* and St Matthew's Church, the spire of which is almost as much of a landmark as that of St John's Kirk. And so, across the end of the High Street, to the offices and the Council Chamber, formerly of the City, and then, since regionalisation, of the District. Designed by a Perth architect Andrew Heiton in neo-Gothic, it dates from 1879. It is not such a happy achievement as some, and one can hardly share the sentiment of a writer of the 1930s who rhapsodised: 'And here today one can see for oneself one of the most beautiful council Chambers that Bonnie Scotland can boast of. There are many larger municipal buildings and many more pretentious civic halls, but both in design and execution this is acknowledged to be a gem above all'. Victorian stained glass windows in the Council Chamber itself depict scenes from Scottish history in Bruce's recapture of Perth from the English, and from Scottish literature in Scott's *Fair Maid of Perth*.

On the wall outside, a moving plaque records how it was

95

placed there by 'the General Officer Commanding, the officers and men of the 1st Polish Army Corps in grateful appreciation of the friendship extended to them in the City and County of Perth where the Polish troops after undergoing many hardships were able to rally and continue with their allies the fight for freedom and liberty 1940–2'. And if that, today, reads sadly, there is an equally sad memorial in the graves of so many Polish soldiers in their war cemetery off the Jeanfield Road in Dovecot Land. Many of their descendants still live in the city and have made names for themselves in various spheres.

CHAPTER SEVEN

The Early Nineteenth Century

It is easy to take stock of the state of Perth at the beginning of the nineteenth century by reading the chapter written by the Rev. J. Scott for Sir John Sinclair's *First Statistical Account*. Though a Borderer by birth and educated at the High School, and then the University, of Edinburgh, Scott nevertheless knew the city well enough after over twenty years' service as minister of St John's Kirk, until, in 1795, his voice (never the strongest part of his equipment as a preacher) finally failed him. Even then, he continued to serve the community—'a sincere Christian, a scholar, a true gentleman, and a lovable man', especially good with boys and young men; for them, we are told, he continued to hold classes in his house in the evenings, always sending each one home with some book to read, on which he might expect to be examined on his next visit. Scott was also a historian, a writer and a prime mover in the founding of the still active Literary and Antiquarian Society of Perth. And a modest man. When writing his Account, he felt a lack of expertise in describing matters of trade and manufacture, and so enlisted the assistance of a small committee of businessmen under a Mr Young.

The picture they painted was of a compact market town serving the surrounding countryside as it had done for centuries, taking in produce for sale or manufacture. As far as manufacture was concerned, the authors unhesitatingly placed Textiles first, both in bulk and in importance. Perth had long been famous for its Silesias or fine linens suitable for handkerchiefs but it also made tougher materials for soldiers' shirts and such things—and also, surprisingly, umbrellas. The trade involved three printfields outside the town and at

Huntingtower and Luncarty 'there is sometimes in the throng of the season, above sixty acres at each, covered with linens'.

Writing in 1794 Scott (or more probably Young) had great hopes of a new development into the cotton trade for which a partnership had been formed which included the inventor Richard Arkwright as well as a Marshall and a Sandeman, but the early failure of this enterprise followed by the general slump of 1810, brought on by Napoleon's blockade, prevented cotton from becoming a serious competitor to linen. And, in any case, it would not be long before textiles would become dependent on steam power rather than water for driving the ever larger machinery; increasingly, such industry would be concentrated where coal was more accessible and the climate wetter, as in Glasgow and Manchester.

Next to linen in importance came leather, another commodity which was handier to get hold of locally. In Perth, 'they prepare at the tan works from 4 to 5000 hides, and about 500 dozen calf skins annually' some for shoes and boots chiefly shipped for the London market Market; some for export unmanufactured; and some for making into gloves, chiefly for the home market.

Salmon was another important export for the London market.

> The fishing begins on the 11th December and ends on the 28th August. The spring and part of the summer fish go fresh, packed on ice . . . and when plentiful in warm weather, they are pickled for the same market. No town in Scotland is better appointed for intercourse with London than Perth, as every four days at least during the fishing season, one smack sails, and in general, makes the passage up within the week, if the weather be in any way favourable.

The minister of the parish of Kinnoull, on the other side of the Tay, goes into even more detail, praising both the abundance and the flavour of the fish to be had, and describing the two large ice-houses that had been built to ensure an adequate supply of that essential commodity. Not much was sold in the town itself because of the low price, ninepence to a shilling a pound, in the spring!

Curiously, Mr Young gives little notice to metalwork which

had featured so largely in the early history of the town and enabled the guild of the Hammermen to acquire prominence; but the smiths can have seldom lacked for work in view of the needs of the farmers; theirs was, in fact, one of the crafts on the verge of a boom with the invention and development of steam power.

Returning to more general matters, Scott is able to praise the manners and morals of Perth's citizens, except for those who patronised the theatre of the day—a rather surprising criticism from one who was well ahead of his day in broad-mindedness (even in ecclesiastical and ecumenical matters)—and the inns, at times when they should have been at their looms or other business. On the whole, he says, the craftsmen have always been distinguished by a strict regard to religion, and by the remarkable care which they took in bringing up their children, their apprentices, and even their journeymen, in good principles and practices, but he adds, a little sadly 'I have heard from some among them that they do not find it a matter so easy to control their young people as it formerly was.'

On the whole, Scott believed Perth to be a healthy place, suggesting as reasons, the protection from east winds provided by Kinnoull Hill and even the demolition of the city walls, in that this brought more air into the city. More likely to have helped would have been better nutrition as a result of the improved farming methods which certainly led to better drainage in the surrounding fields and the elimination of the ague which had plagued so many. More use was made of the potato, and diet amongst the less well off showed an improvement as did a rise in prosperity for most, if not all, of the inhabitants. To prove his thesis, Scott quoted an ex-rector of the grammar school 'who was used to declare that during the forty years in which he taught in the school, there were some of the scholars who died of accidents, but only two by disease.' One wonders about this—the more so as Penny, writing some thirty years later, gives only partial agreement. On the obliteration of ague, he supports Scott; and he welcomes a gradual decline in smallpox as the ministers impressed on the less educated the advantages of Pasteur's discoveries. Skin diseases, as elsewhere in the kingdom, had declined with increased personal cleanliness and cheaper underclothing. But Scott had omitted that most prevalent and deadly disease of the age, cholera—perhaps he took it for granted. Penny, on the other hand, mentions a particularly bad outbreak in 1832 and lists a whole range of steps taken to eliminate it, from killing off all the local pigs and destroying their styes, to providing soup kitchens. So near and yet so far. The problem of providing a purer water supply had not been solved and so a cholera hospital, which was erected, failed in its purpose until a new supply of good water was obtained via a properly filtered well on Moncreiffe Island at the instance of Dr Anderson.

The gifts of this remarkable man as a teacher have already been referred to. If his teaching was sometimes ahead of the ordinary run of his less able pupils, so were his ideas ahead of his fellow practitioners of education. Instead of the tawse we are told (in the *New Statistical Account*):

> There was no reproach, no severity. If a pupil appeared to be inattentive, trifling away his time, and above all, if any symptoms of vice were observed, his method was to send for him, and in private represent to him the great value of knowledge in guiding a man through the difficulties and intricacies of life—the awful dangers of indulging in vicious habits both to body and soul—and then to appeal to the manly and nobler parts of his nature—and after doing all this, in the gentlest and kindliest manner dismiss him by stating his firm conviction that from henceforth he was sure that he would never have to speak to him again in this manner. He thus not only effectually corrected what was wrong, but secured ever after the gratitude and affection of the scholar, who would not willingly again give offence to such a teacher. Such was the aim and end of the whole man to overcome evil with good.

If that tribute does not suggest a very practical man, Anderson's actual achievements demonstrate the contrary. In point of time, the first and, where public order was concerned, the most important was the scheme which he devised for replacing the old-fashioned street lamps (till then lit by whale oil) with gas lamps. Nor was it long before he was able to supply first, churches and workshops, with adequate gas lighting, and then extend the system to points in private houses.

As far as water was concerned, various advisers and engineers had been called on to provide schemes to provide the citizens with something better than access to the polluted lades and the Tay but they had all foundered for one reason or another.

Even Anderson met with difficulties until he hit on a scheme for establishing the 'Round House' waterworks at the foot of Marshall Place which was to rely on a source on Moncreiffe Island transmitted through pipes which passed under the Tay. Not only did he design the system but he was the architect of the elegant classical building in which it was set, and he supervised all the construction himself. His lasting service to the community was to its health; it is only fitting that the design of the building is also a most worthy memorial to himself. He deserved such a one just as Thomas Hay Marshall deserved his tribute (in which, too, Anderson had a hand). Chemist, geologist, mathematician, engineer, architect and politician he has been called, but he was also a God-fearing man and friend of the Rev. Thomas Chalmers and an educational pioneer and a moderate in politics at a time when political passions ran high (1832–3). He could propose the radical Mr Oliphant as candidate for Parliament after the Reform Act without losing the trust of the Tory element. And he was as concerned that schooling should be extended to the children of the less well off as that the paying pupils of his own Academy should get the start in life which would most benefit them and their community. To this end, he started schools for the poor in the Watergate (by now a declining district) and in the New Row at the other end of the city where factories were being built, and, for adults, a Mechanics Institute and Library at which he and his mathematical assistant from the Academy both found time to lecture. Eventually, he received the promotion that was his due and was appointed Professor of Natural Philosophy at St Andrews University, in 1837.

Here he kept his terms dutifully and was beloved by his pupils who appreciated that little bit extra that he gave them, but he preferred to retain his home in Perth where he had married (into The Beautiful Order) the daughter of Provost Ramsay. For a time he lived in one of the new spacious houses on St Leonard's Bank, enjoying the company of his wife and family and, rather unexpectedly, golf. He had been one of the founders of the Royal Golfing Club and even acted as one of the joint directors of the fashionable Social Assemblies.

Unfortunately his last nine years were not the happiest of the life that he had devoted to serving the community. His wife died. His family involved him in financial difficulties. The Church he loved was disrupted. And the higher education which he so passionately believed in was disrupted too by a venomous colleague in the University. Death, which came to him peacefully in 1846, must have come as a mercy.

About the time Anderson left the Academy, and just forty years after Scott had written his *First Statistical Account*, there appeared two further descriptions of the city by two very different authors; the Rev. William Thomson wrote the *Second Statistical Account* (with a preface on Topography and Natural History by 'his very talented scientific friend Dr Adam Anderson')—a useful if somewhat pedestrian work, the very opposite to its contemporary *Traditions of Perth*, a gossipy collection of personal reminiscences by a journalist, George Penny, all mixed up with memories of what he had been told by his father. Penny was an eccentric, described by one who knew him:

> Those who knew George Penny will remember how he pushed his way from Stormont Street to the East Church on Sunday, with his wife hanging on his arm, but trailing a yard behind. He argued the case with her, asserting that, with a fair start, it was quite as easy for her to keep in line with him as to follow a yard after him; but she refused to be convinced, and dangled still. George went on, and although she kept fast hold of his arm, he seemed perfectly unconscious of her presence, and a casual observer would certainly conclude that she belonged to the next group. Mrs Penny's name was Barbara, and her husband used to relate, with an intense glow of waggish recollection, how he was saluted by a street arab as he went

to church the first Sunday after his marriage: 'As I was walking along George Street in big nuptial grandeur, with my light blue coat, velvet neck, and rich basket buttons, my white trousers terminating in an arch over my spotless wellingtons my young bride hanging affectionately on my arm, and both of us calculating that we were bound to make an impression on the gay moving throng, a little ragged urchin screamed from the crown o' the causeway, 'Eh! there goes George Penny, wi' his Bawbee'. 'Yes', said George, 'and that's no the warst o't; for along the same street between us, the little ragged rascal, or another of the same sort, cried, 'Eh! there goes a penny-three-farthings'.

As a boy Penny had been apprenticed to a weaver, a craft from whom many radicals came and, as such, he was a strong critic of 'The Beautiful Order' if indeed he did not invent the phrase; and, naturally, when he found his true *métier* as a journalist, he joined the more radical of Perth's two newspapers, *The Perthshire Advertiser and Strathmore Courier*, as its 'general factotum, reporter, paragraph collector, traveller, machinist, . . . a genial soul, without affectation, beloved by everyone'.

His 'Traditions' chronicle the changes in dress, diet and housing of both rich and poor from his father's day to his, and even their baptismal, marriage and funeral arrangements. He had little sympathy with the large wigs surmounted with cocked hats and the silver-buckled shoes of the wealthy males of the late eighteenth century and the hoop skirts of their ladies, so wide that they had to be lifted head high on one side before going through a door. But in one respect, he could praise his father's days; the lasses then were brought up not in such frivolous accomplishments as learning to play the piano, but were taught the use of the spinning wheel. As the whole of the household linen as well as the blankets were home made, a good supply of these articles was a matter of honest pride with the mother and daughters of a family. The working man had, of necessity, to be content with hard wearing cloth of hodden grey for his coat and waistcoat, short breeches hung without the aid of braces, and homemade stockings. 'In the matter of female dress, there existed as at present a considerable diversity' but the plaid figured largely and, for the married woman, the mutch ornamented for the Sabbath with ribbons. Early in the nineteenth century, breeches increasingly gave way to trousers for men.

In the eighteenth century, the poorer classes made do with porridge and skimmed milk for breakfast; kail or even nettles boiled with pease bannocks or oatcakes for their mid-day meal and much the same for supper, the better-off being able to afford meat and salmon in season; less often, because more expensive, were white fish, salted haddock or codlings from St Andrews. Improvements, when they came, were potatoes and a greater variety of vegetables. Curiously enough Penny does not mention chickens, which certainly were kept because most even of the humbler homes barely furnished within, had some sort of yard or little garden. Tea for the wealthy made its appearance, but was much frowned on by the more conservative and was often resorted to surreptitiously; beer and even whisky were considered far more respectable.

As might be expected, Penny was critical of the amount of money provided by the magistrates at the city's expense to assist the salaries of the teachers at the Academy which existed for those boys whose parents could afford to pay fees while so little was done for the sons of those who could not, a view shared, as we have seen, by Dr Anderson; but he was able to report some progress in the foundation of a Trades School in Mill Street, a Guildry Incorporation school, three little schools in the King James VI Hospital, and even 'various female schools for instructions in needlework and other necessary accomplishments' which must surely have included reading and writing and counting; and he looked forward to the erection of two school houses which it was hoped would give every parent in the city the chance to provide their children with the fundamental branches of education.

If the poorer classes needed better educational facilities, their need for medical help was no less great. Scott's claim that Perth was a healthy city only shows his low expectations. The *Second Statistical Account* dwells on the constant visitations of the Plague in days gone by, and on a virulent epidemic of cholera in 1832; and Penny lists some sixteen diseases which he considers as still common of which ague, consumption, chincough and worms in the stomach he considered as somewhat on the decline, while palsy and apoplexy and certain 'fevers' were on the increase. The first serious attempt to improve matters was the Perth Dispensary of 1819 (largely for vaccination), followed by the laying of the Foundation Stone of an Infirmary to hold 56 patients in County Place. This served its purpose from 1834 until the present Perth Royal Infirmary took its place at the beginning of the twentieth century.

In one respect, however, Perth was both fortunate and ahead of its time. James Murray's 'Royal Asylum for Lunatics' was the product of an extraordinary chain of circumstances. Murray, a day labourer,* had a half brother by his mother's first marriage, who had made a fortune trading in India. This man, William Hope, had decided on health grounds to return to Britain and, with that in view, had altered his will to provide that, if anything should happen to him and his family, his fortune should go to his mother and his half-brothers. In the event, the ship bringing him back sank (with three others) and all were drowned on 30 January 1809. James Murray, having neither wife nor children, left his share to build a fine house in rolling grounds on Kinnoull Hill as an asylum, and endowed it so that 'the meanest patient could be well fed and clothed, and those among the higher classes who could pay for it were as well lodged and cared for as they could be in a palace'. Furthermore, unusually for those days, the managers 'used no coercion, everything is mild. . . . each person has a separate room'. (Penny). The Institution, since greatly enlarged, has retained both its amenities and its reputation to this day.

In the local history section of the Sandeman Library there is a slender bound book containing the regulations laid down for the running of the hospital which makes fascinating reading. The duties of the Superintendent and of the other officials are laid down in great detail, for example:

---

*A day labourer's average wage was one shilling and twopence a day.

The Murray Royal Hospital.

He shall take care that all the patients and servants rise and go to bed the hours prescribed by the by-laws; he shall pay the greatest attention to cleanliness, in the persons, the clothes, and the apartments of the patients. He shall see that the pauper male patients are shaved every third day, the other (paying) patients every second day; that they be all washed every day, and bathed when necessary; that their linens and stockings be changed at least every third day, and oftener when necessary; their flannels once a week; their feet shall be carefully examined every day, particularly in winter.

At the end, just before a detailed list of the clothing provided for each patient comes the diet prescribed for the paupers

Breakfast—Porridge, milk or beer; tea and bread and butter on Sundays.

Dinner—Broth and meat on alternate days; with potatoes and other vegetables; pease soup or potato soup in winter occasionally; fresh fish when plentiful and cheap, may be substituted once or twice a week at the discretion of the matron.

Suppers—Bread and beer; occasionally two ounces of cheese. (a diet which would compare favourably with that of many households in Perth at the time).

Such to be the food of the ordinary patients; but for those who pay a higher board, a more expensive diet shall be provided at the direction of the physician. None to get porter, strong ale, wine or spirits, except those for whom they are particularly ordered.

Crime and punishment were topics that interested the Rev. Dr Thomson. His statistics on the former show that assault and theft were rife—not surprising in those comparatively unpoliced days, but other crimes were few and far between; unfortunately he does not give us any clue as to how many police the magistrates could afford to employ, nor what they were paid, which would have been interesting. But where punishment was concerned he is scathing about the recently completed Town Prison behind the new County Buildings. Its only merit was that it was secure, but the ventilation was insufficient, the cells overcrowded and 'the prisoners allowed to associate daily . . . in a dirty dayroom in complete idleness, thus neutralising all attempts at reformation'. And he goes on to quote a report to the same effect by the Inspector of Prisons for Scotland.

On the other hand he has praise for two of the Bailies, Messers Graham and Dewar, for an experiment on which they have embarked in conjunction with the police in the Old Prison which had previously been the town's only place of confinement until the new one had been built. This had been part of the Tolbooth at the foot of the High Street. Only twenty years before, it had been described by Elizabeth Fry the distinguished prison reformer, after visiting the Depot for the French prisoners of war. Of the Tolbooth she reported (1818):

The Old Jail of Perth, which we inspected . . . is built over a gateway in the middle of the town. Although this dark and wretched building had for some time been disused, as a prison, it was not at the period of our visit without its unhappy inhabitants. We found in it two lunatics in a most melancholy condition; both of them in solitary confinement; their apartments were dirty and gloomy; and a small dark closet connected with each of the rooms was filled up with a bed of straw. In these closets, which are far more like the dens of wild animals than the habitations of mankind, the poor men were lying with very little clothing on them. They appeared in a state of fatuity, the almost inevitable consequence of the treatment to which they were exposed. Noone resided in the house to superintend these

107

afflicted persons, some man living in the town having been appointed to feed them at certain times of day. A few days after our visit one of these poor creatures was found dead in his bed. I suppose it to be in consequence of this event, that the other, though not recovered from his malady, again walks the streets of Perth without control. It is much to be regretted that no medium could be found between so cruel an incarceration, and total want of care.

By 1837 it had been converted into eight separate cells, each provided with a hammock and a seat for its sole occupant; the cells were cleaned daily; the inmates were provided with work (their own trade where this was possible); they were adequately fed and thus enjoyed excellent health, and were precluded from leading one another astray. The whole experiment was conducted at a lesser charge to the community than the communal life in a conventional jail. Unfortunately we do not know whether the experiment was continued when these two enterprising bailies, Graham and Dewar, ended their term of office.

Other developments recorded in the *New Statistical Account* include a steep rise in population from under 15,000 in 1801 to over 20,000 in 1831, producing an extension of the town's boundaries to the north, south and west which is very evident in contemporary maps. There were also new public buildings to record; St Paul's (1807) of which someone acidly remarked that the High Street needed a spire at its head to set it off, and that therefore there had to be a church too;* the very fine Academy building already mentioned, a theatre at the corner of Atholl Street and Kinnoull Street; the classical County Buildings facing the Tay with a county jail behind (1819); Dr Anderson's Gas Works of 1824 and his Waterworks (1830), not to mention the building in George Street of the domed Library (now the Museum) erected by the grateful citizens of Perth to their Provost, Thomas Hay Marshall; and, finally, yet another new church, St Leonards in the Fields. Of a different nature was the 'Depot' which the government built

---

*In fact, it was much needed. St John's was incapable of further extension. And the soldiers from the neighbouring barracks had nowhere to worship.

hurriedly in 1812 on the southern outskirts of the burgh at the expense of £130,000 to house up to 7,000 French prisoners of war—later to be converted into an ordinary prison.

Where trade and industry were concerned, the author finds special mention for a recently opened factory for spinning flax which provided work for 18 boys aged 12–15, 17 girls aged 15–20 and 16 older women, the hours being 69 per week. He rightly observes when discussing education later on that such work left no real opportunity for learning. The factory acts were soon to limit the hours in theory but it was much longer before they were effectively enforced. An entry in the School Log Book for neighbouring Rattray records as late as 1903: 'I find that the halftimers employed in the Keithbank Mill are at present working on their schoolday before and after school; that is to say that a boy spends one day in the mill from 6a.m. to 6p.m. and the next day in the mill from 6a.m. to 8.30a.m., at school from 9.30 to 4.15 and then in the mill from 4.30 to 6p.m.. As a result, such a boy is quite unfit to make progress in his studies'.

Poor communications were another problem. There was as yet no railway to Perth—one of the reasons being that which affected the whole country, the intense reluctance of landowners to allow the dangerous, dirty and unsightly things to pass over their land. Roads had improved between the larger centres of population owing to private enterprise turnpikes, but elsewhere they were still mere tracks. And, as the Tay increasingly silted up, the harbour, once opposite the end of the High Street, had to move eastwards and the total of Perth shipping declined while that of Dundee grew.

One trade which the Reverend author could have enlarged on himself, without calling in expert help, was the book trade of which Perth was a centre throughout the period. He does mention that the town had three lending libraries and more than one newspaper, and he does name a member of the Morison family as editor of the *Courier*, the more Conservative journal, but he hardly does justice to the place of the Morison dynasty in Perth's story.

They stemmed from one Francis Morison 'glazier and

bookbinder', in the second half of the eighteenth century, and also Deacon of the Incorporation of Wrights, whose craft included all who worked with edged tools. Francis's son not only followed his father as a glazier and bookbinder, but became the town's postmaster—and a highly industrious and able one—but also a publisher (of amongst other things a Perth Magazine) and a bookseller. His advertisement read:

> Sold by Robert Morrison, Postmaster in Perth, School Books; Bibles, gilt and plain; Psalm books, ditto; and every book (on a short notice) at the same price as at the place of publication. Writing paper, gilt and plain; Mourning Paper; Message cards; Sealing wax; Red, Black and White wafers; Red, Black, Japan and China ink; Blacklead pencils; Hair pencils; Quills; Pen Knives; Ivory holders; Brass and leather Ink Pieces; Fountain and Thumb Ink glasses; Slates and Slate Pencils; Pounce; Shining Sand; Juniper' Essence of Peppermint; Baume de vie; Turbington's Drops; Lozenges for coughs and colds; Anderson's Pills; Daff's Elixir; Stoughton's Drops; British Oil; Radcliff's Purging Elixir; Dr Bateman's Drops; Balsam of honey; Nipple Ointment; Shining Black Cakes for shoes, which preserve the leather to the last, and do not soil the stockings or fingers; Essence of lemons, which entirely takes out the stains on linen Cambricks or Lawns, etc.
>
> Also Window glass, Books bound in the neatest manner; just from London, a large Collection of little books for Children, Catalogues whereof may be had gratis.

As the copyist remarked, it is a pity that we cannot now see his 'Catalogue of Little Books for Children'.

In succession, Robert's two sons continued the tradition, one as a publisher the other as a printer. And James, in his turn, had four sons, all of whom worked in the same line of printing, publishing, or selling; one of them, David, also acted as Secretary to the Literary And Antiquarian Society and even, like his friend Dr Anderson, turned amateur architect and designed the Rotunda in George Street as a monument to Provost Thomas Hay Marshall. Thereafter the family turned to other avocations, but the tradition which they had started has continued, and to this day, there are no fewer than nine printers listed in the 'yellow pages' of the telephone directory.

In the long run, of course, far the most important event in the first half of the nineteenth century, locally, as well as nationally, was the coming into power of Lord Grey as Prime Minister and the reform of both central and local government which ensued. Curiously, Penny, who gives us graphic accounts of the agitations of the years 1770–1800, the Meal Mobs, the Militia Riots, the Friends of the People and their United Scotsmen (these last two organisations were too extreme and ungodly even for him) gives little attention to the reforms, even though they meant the dissolution for ever of the power of the Beautiful Order to perpetuate itself. Even the Second Statistical Account is brief on the subject, though the writer does mention that Perth did at last send a representative of its own to the House of Commons, elected by all those who owned or rented property to the value of £10 a year—a long way from democracy, but as Professor Ferguson describes it 'a posting stage on the way. . . . and, as such, difficult to operate efficiently.' Influence still played a part, but that was steadily reduced by reform of the Civil Service'. Power now lay in the hands of the middle classes. More revolutionary where the citizens of a still small burgh like Perth were concerned was the creation of a City Council which was genuinely elected by all £10 householders; at the first election only one of the old names was successful, a Sandeman— Thomas Robert, a wine merchant.

The Sandemans were a large family—a clan almost—descended from one David, who came to Perth from Alyth in 1681. One of his sons built up a dyeing business at Luncarty which was carried on by his descendants until the nineteenth century, when it was eventually merged with Pullars. Professor Archibald Sandeman of Manchester, to whom we owe the Sandeman Library, came of that line. Another son, George, lived in the Watergate and was the father of the George who left Perth in 1785 at the age of twenty and went on to found the Portuguese wine firm which did so much to make port a popular as well as a patriotic drink during the Napoleonic Wars. A remarkable feature of the firm was that it only had three heads between its formation and 1923, George until 1841, his nephew until 1868, and then Albert Glas Sandeman until 1923.

Other Sandemans distinguished themselves in distant parts of the world and have included a General, a member of the Board of the Bank of England and a Moderator of the Church of Scotland. Yet they have seldom wholly severed their links with Perth and often were brought back to be buried in the Greyfriars burial ground.

Two other distinguished sons of Perth—though they founded no dynasties and made their names overseas—may fitly close this chapter, since both continued to regard Perth as home and are commemorated there—Lord Lynedoch and David Douglas. The former, an aristocrat with liberal leanings, did not become a soldier until he was 45 and yet rose to the rank of General under the Duke of Wellington. The latter was a self-educated gardener's boy who left school at 11 but is remembered to this day as one of the greatest of all botanical explorers.

Lord Lynedoch was born in 1748, plain Thomas Graham, 3rd son of the Laird of Balgowan, with no particular prospects until his two brothers predeceased him. Nor was his first entry into public life particularly promising. He stood for the parliamentary seat of Perthshire against the Tory brother of the Duke of Atholl and lost; even when he was, later, elected to the House of Commons, he made no special mark as a politician. He was far more interested in the hunting field where he was regarded as reckless in the extreme, as indeed he was in his everyday life; he would tour his estates never opening a gate but clearing everything in front of him. On one occasion we are told that he rode from Perth to Edinburgh without once asking for a toll bar to be lifted for him, and that, on another, he made his horse swim him across the Tay when the ferryman refused to launch the ferry boat because the current was too swift. On the plus side however, he earned high praise from the surveyor Robertson as an 'improving' landlord who improved the local cattle by bringing in bulls from Devonshire and Bakewell's sheep from Leicestershire; and he insisted on his tenants observing a carefully planned rotation of crops. But the really memorable event of the first half of his life was his marriage to one of the famous beauties of the day, Mary Cathcart. Her portrait is one of the finest of Gainsborough's and hangs in the National Gallery of Scotland to which it was bequeathed on condition that it never left Scotland. Seventeen years of mutual devotion and great happiness followed, in spite of the marriage being childless. Then a wasting disease carried off the still young and beautiful Mrs Graham in the south of France where she and her husband were seeking a cure for her. He was inconsolable; and when French revolutionaries broke open her coffin while it was being brought home for burial (on the grounds that it might contain contraband) his rage knew no bounds.

Having now nothing left to live for but to hate the French he decided to become a soldier in spite of his age and lack of experience. He obtained leave to raise a regiment in Perthshire at his own expense, mustering it on the North Inch—the 90th—later the 2nd Battalion of the Cameronians. He served at the capture of Minorca, and of Malta; in the retreat to Corunna with Sir John Moore whom he admired enormously, insisting that his own regiment should be trained on Moore's light infantry principles. Under Wellington, he commanded the British troops at the capture of Barossa (hence Barossa Place and Barossa Terrace in Perth). During the crossing of the Pyrenees and in France, he was designated to succeed Wellington if anything should happen to the Commander-in-Chief. He was promoted General in 1809 when he was 62, K.C.B. in 1812 and given a peerage as Lord Lynedoch in 1814, taking his title from a neighbouring estate which he had added to Balgowan. Ill health forced him to retire before Waterloo but he recovered and lived on to be present—on horseback—aged 94, on the occasion when Queen Victoria and Prince Albert visited Perth in 1842. According to Arthur Bryant he was 'perhaps the greatest of all Wellington's commanders in the Peninsula'. His regiment ceased to exist with the Cameronians at a period of military retrenchment in the mid-twentieth century but they, and he, have their memorial at the south east-corner of the North Inch. He is buried in the mausoleum that he built for his wife in Methven churchyard.

When David Douglas was a rebellious urchin tramping the

six miles everyday from his home to school in Kinnoull, he can little have guessed that his last resting place would have been in Honolulu. It was not the six miles that he resented for it was a country walk, and he was fascinated by everything in nature, but the lessons at the end of the walk, and it was a relief to all when, at the age of eleven, he was allowed to leave school and take a job as an apprentice garden boy at Scone Palace. At last he was doing something that interested him. The head gardener soon recognised his exceptional ability and he and his assistant gave the boy all their experience, as also did the Brown brothers, nurserymen in Perth. David himself began to read widely and even went back to school voluntarily when he had finished his apprenticeship to improve his mathematics and learn some science. From there he went to a job near Culross in 1818 in what was probably the finest collection of exotic plants in Scotland at that time. Here he came to the notice of William Hooker (then Professor of Botany at Glasgow University but later to revolutionise Kew Gardens) and Hooker became almost a second father to him, taking him on long botanical expeditions to the Highlands. So impressed was Hooker by his energy, stamina, ability and sobriety that he recommended him to the Horticultural Society in London as a potential explorer and botanical collector.

Douglas's first trip in 1823 was to the, as yet, largely unsettled west coast of North America, and this proved so successful that he was sent back the next year (in a sailing ship around Cape Horn) to scour what are now the states of Washington and Oregon, and the province of British Columbia, west of the Rocky Mountains. Here he reckoned he travelled 3,932 miles, on foot and by canoe, under conditions which were often hazardous, as may be seen from the following extract from his journal, recently transcribed by A.G. Harvey in his book *Douglas of the Forests*. There is no more fascinating reading to anyone interested in adventure or in botany:

> 1826. Friday March 24th. After a tedious night, daybreak was to me particularly gratifying, as might well be guessed, being surrounded by at least 450 savages who, judging from appearances, were

everything but amicable. As none in the brigade could converse with them better than myself, little could be done by persuasion. However finding two of the principal men who understood the Chinook tongue, with which I am partially acquainted, the little I had, I found on this occasion very useful . . . We took a little breakfast on the rocks at Dallas, four miles below the Great Falls, at seven o'clock. The day was very pleasant, with a clear sky. At five in the evening we made the portage over the Falls, where we found the Indians very troublesome. I learnt from Mr Macleod they had collected for the purpose of pillaging the boats which we soon found to be the case. After they had had the usual present of tobacco, they became desirous of our camping there for the night, no doubt expecting to achieve their purpose. The first thing that was observed was their cunningly throwing water on the gun locks, and on the boats being ordered to put into the water, they refused to allow them. As Mr Macleod was putting his hand on one of their shoulders to push him back, a fellow immediately pulled from his quiver a bow and arrows, and presented it at Mr Macleod. As I was standing on the outside of the crowd I perceived it and, as no time was to be lost, I instantly slipped the cover off my gun, which at the time was charged with buckshot, and presented it at him, and invited him to fire his arrow, and then I certainly would shoot him. Just at this time a chief of the Kyeuuse tribe and three of his young men, who are the terror of all other tribes west of the mountains and great friends of the white peoples, as they call them, stepped in and settled the matter in a few words without any further trouble. This very friendly Indian, who is the finest figure of a man that I have seen, standing nearly 6 feet 6 inches high, accompanied us a few miles up the river, where we camped for the night, after being remunerated by Mr Macleod for his friendship— I being King George's Chief or the Grass Man as I am called, I bored a hole in the only shilling I had—one which had been in my pocket since I had left London, and, the septum of his nose being perforated, I suspended it to it with a brass wire. This was to him the great seal of friendship.

After smoking, he returned to the Indian village and promised that he would not allow us to be molested. Of course no sleep was to be had that night, and to keep myself awake I wrote a letter to Dr Hooker. Heavy rain during the night. The following day, the 25th, at daylight we resumed our route; sleet and rain, with a keen north wind. Being almost benumbed with cold, I preferred walking along the bank of the river, and, although my path in many places was very rugged, I camped forty miles above the Falls much fatigued. During the night and the following morning I found my knee troublesome and very stiff.

Sadly, the ability which Douglas had shown in getting on well with the Indians, both hostile and friendly, and with the rough trappers and other pioneers on the frontiers of civilisation, was not evident when he returned to England in 1827. Here, he soon felt undervalued and under-rewarded and he was not happy until he was off on his travels again. His last, and in some ways his most productive voyage of all was in 1829 to British Columbia and California. After one early disaster when his canoe was smashed to pieces and he lost many seeds and specimens, he was able to send back three chests of seeds including those of *Pinus Nobilis* which he considered the noblest of all his finds. Eventually his health, and particularly his eyesight, began to deteriorate, and he moved on to Honolulu from where he hoped to catch a ship home. Here too he found plenty to discover and describe, until final disaster overtook him. He fell into a pit dug for the purpose of entrapping wild cattle and was gored to death by an enraged bull.

To him we owe not only the many species of fir, including the one named after him, but also the introduction to Europe of many garden plants now common, such as lupins, antirhinums, phlox, penstemons clarkias and Californian poppies.

CHAPTER EIGHT

The Later Nineteenth Century

Progress is evolutionary rather than revolutionary, and cannot really be chopped up into periods. The Victorian period did not begin suddenly in 1837 nor end abruptly when the Queen died. Of course a few events in history have brought sudden far-reaching changes, such as the French Revolution and the two World Wars, but the smaller the scale on which one is working, the less like it is that you can speak of specific periods. Nevertheless, the fifty years from 1850 to 1900 do produce a very different Perth; they are less parochial, more outward-looking years. Sandeman and Douglas were exceptions in making their names overseas at the turn of the century, and, in some ways, Lord Lynedoch, but Perth's home-based industries hardly extended beyond Scotland as yet. After that date, Pullars built up what was for a time almost a monopoly in dry-cleaning and dyeing for the whole of the United Kingdom, and Dewars and Bells established themselves first in England and then worldwide. All three were greatly assisted by the coming of the railways, which also did much to change life in Perth and became for a time the largest single employers of labour in the town.

So far as dyeing was concerned, the story starts with the firm of P. and P. Campbell, founded by a Peter Campbell in 1814 in New Row. According to Peter Baxter's *Perth's Old Time Trades and Trading* he gained his experience the hard way:

> He went to London at the age of nineteen to acquire further knowledge in connection with dyeing. There were no railways in those days, and as steamboats were expensive, he sailed in a smack, taking seven days to go from Dundee to Gravesend, and then to London. He had 17/6 in his pocket. He got 24/- for his first week of

work of 72 working hours—6 a.m. till 8 p.m., no Saturday half holiday. Out of his pay he saved 12/- each week. After a time he went to Paris to further improve himself in his trade. Paris was worse than London—6 a.m. till noon; 1 p.m. to 8; Saturday and Sunday alike. He tossed a penny as to whether he would go to America or Ireland but Ireland was stricken with a potato famine and instead he returned to Perth to join his father in his business—very small to start with but steadily expanding as a result of hard work, quick handling of goods and the use of the best dyes.

Only ten years later than 1814, another firm with a name that was to become even more famous, was started up in Perth by John Pullar, son of a textile manufacturer who, some say, had learned the trade with the Campbells. Starting with a staff of six, he contrived over a long life to build up a business which by the end of the century was Perth's largest employer; 2,000 were employed at his works in Kinnoull Street and a further 1,500 as agents throughout the United Kingdom, until the name of Pullars was synonymous with dyeing and cleaning. Eventually, they merged with their rivals after P. and P. Campbell had suffered a disastrous fire in 1919 and shortly after with the London firm of Eastmans . . . Up till then, both had remained one-family firms with the succession passing from father to son. Their works, like others, were strategically placed to draw plenteous supplies of water from the lade—and to discharge effluent into it.

The eldest son of the founder became Sir Robert Pullar, Lord Provost and Member of Parliament. A tribute to him and to the good industrial relations in the firm is a plaque in Kinnoull Street, placed there by his employees to commemorate his jubilee as a partner in the company.

Just about the time that Pullars was beginning to make its name locally, so another industry had its small beginnings which would make the name of Perth known worldwide. In 1864 a young man, John MacDonald Fraser joined the auctioneers' firm of MacDonald and McCallum. He became a partner twelve years later and then managing director, which he remained for 76 years, changing both the name of the firm (to MacDonald Fraser) and the direction of its business to the

Interior of Campbell's Dyeworks, Perth. The company was taken over by Pullars in 1919 (*Reproduced by permission of Perth and Kinross District Council Museums and Art Galleries Department, Scotland*).

sale of pure-bred cattle. Two of his sons followed him and as recently as 1987, a grandson.

Originally the sales took place in the centre of the town but, as business grew and livestock predominated, a new site was found in the Caledonian road, 1875, which was much handier for the railway, and served its purpose for over a hundred years until 24 Oct 1989. Here the famous Bull Sales used, at first, to take place over two weeks in the spring; Aberdeen Angus being shown and sold during the first week and Shorthorn during the second; later there were sales twice a year in both spring and autumn, each lasting four days. The previous judging of the beasts, always well attended by the public and a great excitement, took place—until 1947—in the open. Caledonian Road was roped off and sanded from York Place to Marshall Street. Prices varied throughout the years, dropping during the 1914 War and again in the slump of the thirties but soared again, especially for the Aberdeen Angus in the 1960s. More recently still, the market has also been a main centre for the sale of Continental breeds, Charolais, Simmental and Limousin. The original family firm became part of United Auctions in 1962 but still has a grandson of the founder as its managing director. Recently, the old market—so long a landmark in Perth—has been demolished and moved to extensive new premises on the western outskirts of the city. A supermarket has taken its location.

Neither dyeing nor the bull sales could have prospered but for the railway and the way in which the developers found Perth to be the natural centre for communication and, as such, an ideal place to site their local workshops. The first line to reach the outskirts of the city was that from Dundee to Barnhill on the northern bank of the river in 1847. Two years later a wooden bridge was built over the Tay (with one span that opened to allow ships to get upstream to the then landing place at Commercial Street). In fact, this facility proved less necessary than was expected, since commercial traffic was declining and the pleasure steamers increasingly used the modern harbour downstream of the railway crossing. One problem that did arise for the railway was to secure a large enough stretch of flat land for a station. This led to a violent controversy and nearly to disaster when the Town Council decided to offer the South Inch. Fortunately it proved unsuitable owing to the floodable nature of the land and the difficulties involved by the difference in level between the height of the bridge and that of the Inch itself. In any case there was strong hostility from the citizens at the thought of losing their meadows, and they were ably led by Sheriff-Clerk James Murray Patton—yet another benefactor from the Marshall family, since he was the nephew of Thomas Hay Marshall and the ultimate heir to the latter's fine estate out at Glenalmond.*

Other lines soon followed and, by 1870, no fewer than six converged here, while a seventh was soon added when Glen Farg was opened up as a direct route to Edinburgh. Traffic increased not only for necessary travel and for freight, but also for sightseeing; railway guide books were written telling the traveller what to look out for from his carriage window as he proceeded on his somewhat leisurely way—that is until the motor car brought yet further change.

Even before the Beeching era, the line west to Methven and Crieff was closed, and, more recently, the direct line to Edinburgh via Glenfarg to facilitate the building of the M90 motorway. Most serious of all has been the closure of the railway workshops, which, with the station, employed over 2,000. The industries of lasting growth were to be other than these—those of whisky and insurance which both really took off from the 1890s.

The first John Dewar came from Dull to take charge of a wine storehouse in 1828. Working hard, he managed to set up on his own in the High Street, where Woolworths is today, as a wholesale wine and spirit merchant. As yet his business was local and the whisky he sold was unblended, and sold in keys or jars rather than bottles—grain whisky from the lowlands which sold retail at about a penny a gill! Expansion did not come until his elder son John Alexander succeeded to the management, and the younger, Thomas, went off to

*(opposite) James Murray Patton is remembered with gratitude by generations as the donor of the land on which Glenalmond College was built. Otherwise his inheritance did not prove a happy one. He had no son and neither had his next brother, while the third and last also died childless—a ghastly death within days of inheriting. The cleverest of the three of whom it was said that 'his talents as an advocate, his assiduous application to business, and his singular urbanity and kindness soon raised him in his profession, not only as a pleader in court, but as a consulting counsel'. Having been Lord Advocate, he was raised to the bench in 1868 as Lord Justice Clerk. Only one year later, he went out of Glenalmond house one morning about eight o'clock to take his usual walk before breakfast. It was four days before his body was retrieved from the river Almond, just below Buchanty spout, with his throat cut. Charges which had been made against his election agents over possible bribes having been offered at a previous election campaign, which he fought to retain his constituency of Bridgewater, had probably preyed on his sensitive mind. These, coupled with the position he now held and the recent loss of his last brother, may have contributed but he was never found to be in any way at fault, and he was widely mourned as a liberal landlord and a sympathising neighbour and friend.

London to extend the firm's markets there and to convert the English from their brandy and gin drinking habits. To this end, the grain whiskies were blended with Highland malts and then bottled. For a time this was done in Speygate but, as larger and larger premises were needed a massive complex was built where the Glasgow road intersects with Riggs Road and Glover Street. Eventually even this did not meet the needs of the firm (by now merged with the Distillers Company) and in 1961 yet a new complex was opened at Inveralmond, alongside the Dunkeld road as it leaves the city. Since then there has been the take-over by Guinness.

John Alexander had been made Lord Forteviot in 1917 and his brother Lord Dewar in 1919. Like so many of Perth's successful sons, both were great benefactors—to the restoration of St John's Kirk, to the building of a new wing at Perth Royal Infirmary and a lodging house in the Skinnergate, and the creation of a charitable trust for the benefit of Perth's disadvantaged; and to the purchase for the town of that wonderful area of natural beauty, Kinnoull Hill.

The expansion and modernisation of Perth's whisky industry was not the work of Dewar's alone. They had a formidable rival in that of Bell's. The founders of the two firms had been contemporaries as well as rivals, and there is an apocryphal story about them which is too good to omit. They were both due to attend a church meeting one morning and, finding themselves too early, decided to have a little refreshment. 'What will you have?' said Bell (or Dewar, according to your sympathies). 'A Bell's'. replied Dewar. 'It would hardly do to go into the meeting smelling of whisky.'

The first Arthur Bell had also started in a small way, as a traveller for a firm run by a member of the Sandeman family in the Watergate which sold not only whisky and wine but also tea. He became a partner in 1851 and acquired sole control in the 1860s, moving to Kirkgate, and then, when he needed larger premises, to Victoria Street. Again it was the second generation which managed to extend the business world-wide, in the person of his son Arthur K. Bell. Never Lord Provost (as was Lord Forteviot) and never ennobled, he was yet one of Perth's most widely loved and distinguished citizens, and was made an honorary Freeman of the city together with Lord Amulree and Lord Tweedsmuir. On that occasion, he declared: 'I have been twice across America, through a considerable part of Europe, and three times through Australia and New Zealand, and I have failed to find one spot which I would prefer to live in than our "Fair City".'

He was a quiet man who preferred a simple life, devoted to the welfare of his fellow men; a great lover of all games as a young man, he wanted, as he grew older, to make it possible for those who were like-minded to have the same opportunities of outdoor enjoyment that he had had. Even while building his business, he continued to take an active part in the Perth Cricket Club and made a century at the age of 55. Five years earlier, in 1930, he had bought the then open fields of Gannochy, just across the Coupar Angus road from his home at Kincarrathie House. There he made the cricket ground of Doocot Park and gradually built the housing estate of Gannochy, starting with cottages that could be let at a low rent to (amongst others) railwaymen who had been made redundant in those hard times. Sadly he had no son to carry on his good work and so, two years before he died, he set aside a considerable part of his shareholding in the company to create the Gannochy Trust with a view to helping the citizens of Perth, especially the young and the old. When his widow died, the trust converted his residence into a Home for the elderly. They contributed £600,000 towards a new sewage system for the town, £500,000 for twelve flatlets and a work centre for spastics and, amongst countless other benefactions, built the magnificent Sports Centre on the North Inch, and later extended it greatly. This last provides facilities for 5-a-side football, indoor hockey, volleyball, tennis, badminton gymnastics, keep-fit, indeed the whole range of indoor activities. It is open to visitors as well as local members (and widely used by them in the summer) on a day-to-day basis though only members can book facilities in advance. Large grants have also been made to neighbouring institutions, such as £125,000 for a new hall of residence at St Andrews

University, and gifts to those of Stirling and Strathclyde, and to schools and also organisations helping the elderly. And apart from the trust, the firm of Bells' have also recently built new tennis and squash courts for the Perth Tennis Club in Hay Street. At one time the largest independent whisky company in the country, Bells is now part of United Distillers.

The third of the commercial ventures to which Perth owes so much, and which is now its biggest employer, is the General Accident Fire and Life Assurance Corporation. Here too the start was in quite a small way, as a response to the obligations imposed by the Employers' Liability Act in 1880. A group of local men—an agricultural Engineer, a farmer, a banker, a lawyer, a doctor, a butcher, a brewer (one almost expects to find a baker and a candlestick maker) joined together since they did not see why the premiums which they had to pay should go out of the neighbourhood. Had that been all, their venture might have been shortlived, but they had the wisdom to appoint as their manager an able young man who was determined to 'go places'—and *did*, Francis Norie-Miller.

At that time, the big fire and life companies were already well established, and he saw that he must look to specialise in other fields such as burglary insurance and motor cover, as well as accident and fire. But, before he took the job, Norie-Miller had had to overrule his father's opposition, who told him he was making a mistake in giving up the safe job and excellent prospects as assistant manager with an already established firm. 'I feel I can control; I want a company to control'. In fact, he could not only control; he could infuse his own tremendous energy into all who worked with him. Within a year he had opened a number of branches throughout the country and secured 800 agents. Within four years, the capital of the company had increased from £2,500 to £100,000. He travelled untiringly all over Britain, 25,000 miles in the first year, and he had a flair for seeing new lines of business which might prove profitable. He was first into the field of burglary insurance in 1890; motor insurance in 1896; and later in no-claims bonuses, and was among the first in householders' comprehensive insurance. In early days, he insisted that every claim should be settled on the day that it was adjusted, and accompanied it with a personal letter. He travelled all over the world to establish General Accident worldwide until two-thirds of the premiums came from overseas.

Sadly, his eldest son was killed in the First World War, but the second, Stanley, returned safely (having won a Military Cross) and he changed from a career in law to join the company. In due course, he succeeded his father as general manager and then as chairman, and the company has continued to grow. Today it employs more than 15,000 people, over 1,000 of them in Perth, where its head office has always remained, although its needs have long outstripped its original premises in Tay Street. That has been retained as a sort of museum, and houses some of its earliest records, but its main HQ has been transferred, very recently, to a vast complex most skilfully designed to fit into the hillside at Cherry Bank.

Like A.K. Bell, both Sir Francis and his son Sir Stanley were made honorary freemen of the city, and, in memory of the latter, a beautiful riverside walk and garden have been created on the bank of the river opposite the original premises.

Outside the business community, one of Perth's most distinguished sons was the Rev John Watson D.D., alias Ian Maclaren. It is true that he spent much of his life in Liverpool serving there at Sefton the vocation that had called him to the Free Church ministry, but his most formative, and the happiest years, were spent as a boy at Perth Academy and then when, at the outset of his ministry, he received a call to serve those who adhered to the Free Church in neighbouring Glenalmond.

As a minister, his strength was as a pastor rather than a preacher. Indeed, in his earliest days he was too often told that he would never make a preacher, but 'he showed', wrote his biographer 'extraordinary determination in the art of preaching without manuscript'.

Although he sometimes wondered in after years whether the practice had not overstrained his brain, he seldom entered the pulpit with anything but a page of notes and heads. Sometimes in these early days his memory would fail. 'Friends' he would say, 'that is not very clear. It was clear in my study on Saturday, but now I will begin again.' These good country people never showed impatience, and a gaunt Highland elder came to him after service one Sunday and said, 'When you are not remembering your sermon just give out a psalm and we will be singing that while you are taking a rest, for we are all loving you and praying for you.' The Logiealmond days were days of real happiness for him. He looked back at them with constant tenderness. He loved the country and he knew the country folk. He amazed his parishioners with his knowledge of crops, cattle and corn markets, and all the details.*

It was these folk who, towards the end of his life, gave him the inspiration for his first two books, *Beside the Bonnie Brier Bush* and *Days of Auld Lang Syne*, sketches of rural life in a remote glen. The title of the former came from a line in one of James Hogg's Jacobite songs: 'There grows a bonnie brier bush on oor kailyard'

'I chose this title' he said 'because the suggestion of the book is that in every garden, however small and humble, you may have a flower . . . This is the whole idea of my writing, to show the rose in places where many people only look for cabbages'. Hence the appellation of the 'Kailyard School' given to Barrie, Crockett and himself.

His first book, with its combination of humour and pathos and skilful character drawing (almost entirely through dialogue) was an immediate success, and though the sentimentality is now out of fashion, the tales are still attractive to read for someone who knows the countryside. And, if the picture he painted seems too idealised, it was not from ignorance of the grim realities of work on some farms; as a boy, he had spent many holidays working on his uncles's farms where, at harvest times, he had witnessed scenes he said, beside which even *The House with the Green Shutters* would have seemed mild.

The other book of Watson's which still lives on today is his

---

*Robertson Nicoll. *Ian Maclaren. The Life of the Rev John Watson D.D.*, Hodder and Stoughton, 1908.

Young Barbarians, a book meant for boys in the tradition of *Tom Brown's Schooldays*. The story is set unmistakably in the buildings and surroundings of the old Perth Academy on the North Inch, though some of the characters were probably influenced by people he remembered from Stirling where he finished his schooling. It is perhaps the dominies who come most sharply to life and remain in one's memory, but there is an understanding of boy nature too, as it really is, and not as other Victorian clerics felt it ought to be. Fun abounds and there is an absence of preaching. Try it!

It will no doubt have been noticed that, apart from references to the benefactions of Lord Dewar and A.K. Bell, those parts of modern Perth which lie on the east bank of the Tay have barely received a mention. Until Thomas Smeaton built his substantial bridge over the river in the 1770s, the districts of Bridge End, Kinnoull, and Barnhill were quite separate little villages with access to Perth only by the ferry at Kincarrathie or that which plied from the foot of South Street; but the land all belonged to the Hays, Earls of Kinnoull.

The 1st Earl was one of the 'middling sort of people' on whom James VI relied in order to avoid becoming too heavily dependent on those over-mighty subjects who had so often frustrated—and sometimes even got rid of his predecessors— 'hangable men' he called them. George Hay had been present at Gowrie House on the day when the Gowries were so summarily disposed of, and he had supported the King's story in the subsequent trial. As a result, he was taken into the King's favour* which he retained by falling in with the King's ecclesiastical policies, notably the episcopalian Five Articles of Perth. By 1622 he was Lord Chancellor of Scotland and, in due course, he was made an earl. His duties and his adherence to the Court meant that he spent little time in his house in the Watergate and much more in Edinburgh and London. James was well enough satisfied with his work but

---

*Among others who gained by supporting James after this affair was David Murray whose descendants, the Earls of Mansfield and Mansfield, still own the lands of Scone with which they were rewarded.

Charles I wanted a stronger Anglican and, when he visited Edinburgh in 1633 expected his Archbishop of Canterbury to take precedence over all Scottish dignitaries including the Lord Chancellor of Scotland. Time-server though Hay was, he would have none of that on his home ground and declared that 'never a stolled priest should set a foot before him in Scotland so long as his blood was hot'. After a brief unseemly squabble, Charles felt it wiser to yield, saying that he would 'meddle no further with that gouty, cankered old man from whom is nothing to be gathered but sour words'. Charles also probably felt that he would not have to for long and, in fact,

Tomb of the First Earl of Kinnoull (1635), in Old Kinnoull Church.

Hay did die the following year. His corpse was shipped home and buried in the family vault of the old Kinnoull Church in which Margaret Tudor, widow of James IV, had been married to her second husband. This vault is all that remains now of that church, but it houses one of the most elaborate Renaissance tombs in Scotland, with a standing statue of the Lord Chancellor in one of its partitions and the bag to contain the Great Seal in the other.

The aisle and the little burial ground lie opposite the entrance to Manse Road, between the Dundee Road and the river. For long a derelict area, the burial ground is about to be smartened up as part of the riverside walk; it contains some interesting headstones, including one depicting a ferryman in his boat, and several showing the craft emblems of the deceased. There is also the family lair of the Grays of Bowerswell who included Effie, wife in turn to Ruskin and to Sir John Everett Millais R.A. Best of all the Perth and Kinross Heritage Trust is to undertake the preservation of the earl's tomb.

Kinnoull Hill, up behind, was bought from the Hay family in 1923 by Lord Dewar, and endowed and presented to the people of Perth, providing them with yet another amenity, comparable to those of the two Inches. Here is a place to walk through woods which part at intervals to reveal really wonderful views to all points of the compass* The 9th Earl liked to entertain his friends to picnics on the summit and built there a stone table and a tower—a folly to imitate those towers which rise above the River Rhine. Further along, his neighbour, Lord Gray, from Kinfauns, built another. Not far from the tower and the table is one of two mountain indicators packed with information about what can be seen. But perhaps the best view of all is that from the tower, over Kinfauns Castle, to the broad Tay as it winds its way to Dundee and the sea. To the south is the equally fine Moncreiffe Hill and the

*An admirable leaflet and plan prepared by the Forestry Commission, who share the management with the Perth and Kinross District Council, may be obtained free from the Tourist Office in the High Street.

Lomonds of Fife, and, to the west, Strathearn. Only to the north, towards the Grampians, is the vista restricted by the trees. In this direction, a rather more extended expedition is needed—to the high ground above the new Murrayshall golf course or to Dunsinane Hill or the King's Seat.

Kinnoull Hill may be approached from a number of routes easily picked out on the map, but the two most convenient are from the end of Bowerswell Road and Hatton Road, and from the Jubilee car park off the Muirhall Road. The former is the more direct and leads on to the Nature Trail to but it is rather steeper; the latter provides half-an-hour's easy walking along paths and gradients that a septuagenarian with a seven-year-old can negotiate; it is well signposted to the Tower and to the Table, just beyond.

Kinnoull Hill is now covered on its lower slopes with pleasant houses but it was not until the nineteenth century that Perth's wealthier citizens came to appreciate the charms of living across the river, first along its banks above Perth Bridge, and then on the higher ground. Most of the earlier mansions with gardens running down to the river are now, alas, offices, but there is one interesting, new, house lived in by Mr Ian MacArthur when he was M.P. for East Perthshire, and, at Upper Springlands, some flats for the physically handicapped, administered by the Scottish Council for Spastics; both have wonderful views across the North Inch. Springlands itself was the home of Mrs Stewart Sandeman, a remarkable lady who personified much of Victorian Perth and Perthshire. Her Stewart father owned the estate of Bonskeid on Loch Tummel but was also a doctor practising in Perth from his home in the Watergate where his daughter grew up; she was old enough to remember buying trinkets from the French prisoners of war in the Perth Prison. Her mother was an Oliphant from Gask and sister to the Jacobite poetess Caroline, Lady Nairne; and she married Mr Glass Sandeman who united those two Perth names. She herself joined the Free Church at the time of the Disruption and devoted her life to evangelism and good works without losing any of her charm or her enjoyment of life, a tradition which she handed on to her descendants, one of whom (from Fincastle which she also inherited) subsequently became Moderator of the Church of Scotland.

Yet another new building set in a pleasant garden is one that housed for a time the computer facilities of General Accident, but has now been turned to other uses. All these may be reached by the A93 which goes on to Scone Palace and the Race Course, Stobhall, Kinclaven Bridge, the site of a Roman Camp at Inchtuthil, the great beech hedge at Meikleour, Ardblair Castle and Newton Castle above Blairgowrie.

The A94 goes out between Kincarrathie House and Doocot Park on the left and the Gannochy estate on the right. It is a busy road, carrying heavy traffic to Aberdeen, pretty enough at certain times of year but not to be recommended for pleasure, except for getting to such places as Glamis and Kirriemuir and the highland country north of Alyth.

If instead of turning left after Perth Bridge, you go straight up Lochie Brae into Muirhall Road, you pass the Murray Royal Hospital and eventually reach the Jubilee Car Park and access to Corsie Hill, the Kinfauns Forest Walks and Kinnoull Hill.

Turning right along Gowrie Street, there are several roads off to the left, up the hill. Bowerswell Road leads past the house of that name into Hatton Road. The house was one of the earlier buildings and was occupied for a time by John Ruskin's grandfather, then by a Mr Gray, father of Euphemia, or Effie as she was known. In due course, Ruskin, who had also spent part of his boyhood in Perth, on the other side of the river in a house in Rose Terrace, was married to Effie in the drawing room of Bowerswell House; but he wanted a companion, not a wife, and the marriage was desperately unhappy for both. When, eventually, she found someone she could love and be loved by, in the person of James Everett Millais, the Pre-Raphaelite painter, she was able to get a decree of nullity and marry Millais. After the Second World War, the house was converted into homes for the elderly. A descendant of Effie's brother was largely responsible

Bowerswell House, where Ruskin married Effie Gray.

for the acquisition of the present peal of bells in St John's Kirk.

Hatton Road leads past a Roman Catholic monastery of the Redemptorist Fathers to the start of the Kinnoull Nature Trail.

Yet further along the Dundee Road is the Isle of Skye Hotel, the oldest part of which used to be the Kinnoull schoolmaster's house with, adjoining it, the little school, still with its niche for the bell to summon children to school. The children of the modern school and their teacher Miss Fothergill compiled a most informative little book on the area 1973–4 full of old stories—it is still on sale. Amongst others, David Douglas was a pupil there in the first decade of the 19th century, walking all the way from Scone each day.

Finally, before leaving the town, there is a notice directing you to the National Trust for Scotland's *Branklyn Garden*. This has been described as the 'finest two acres of garden in the country' and should on no account be missed. Here lived from 1922–67 the wife of Mr John Renton, and here, supported by her husband, she created a dream through which one can wander along paths between azaleas and rhododendrons and every rare shrub, sheltered by taller trees, up and down little braes, with little lawns and screes with rockery plants. For the expert there are countless rarities to which a guide can be purchased, while for the less knowledgeable, there are the sheets of colour provided in abundance by the shrubs, the mecanopsis and the lilies and hydrangeas. Though standing high, its southern aspect enables it to grow many plants that it is surprising to find so far north on the eastern side of Scotland. April, May and June are the best months but there is much to enjoy at any time of year.

Shortly after the road bends at Branklyn, there is a little road to the right which leads to the river. There you will find the Perth Sailing Club, established some forty five years ago, principally involved in dinghy sailing. A water-ski club operates from the harbour.

Astride the A 85 to Dundee, there is much rich farming land and a string of castles and gracious houses but they are mostly still in private occupation and not normally open to the public. Two, however call for special mention in case the visitor is fortunate enough to be in Perth on the day on which their gardens are open to the public under the Scottish Gardens Scheme—Rossie Priory and the unique glades of the Cox family at Glendoick, once the home of Duncan Forbes, Lord Advocate at the time of the '45 and, later, Lord President of the Court of Session.

Only Kinfauns Castle falls within Perth itself. Though it is not an ancient building it has an interesting history. The first well-recorded owners were the Charteris family who played a considerable, and sometimes noisy, part in Perth's history during the 15th and 16th centuries. From them, it passed (through the Blairs) to the Grays of Fowlis Easter, another exceedingly turbulent family. The 1st Lord Gray conspired against James I; the 2nd Lord Gray *with* James II to murder

Perth Harbour. Oil on canvas. By an unknown artist, *c.* 1890 (*Reproduced by permission of Perth and Kinross District Council Museums and Art Galleries Department, Scotland*).

the Earl of Douglas; the 6th against both Mary Queen of Scots and James VI. It was the 12th who married Margaret Blair and so came into the Kinfauns estate, and the 15th who built 1820–2 the vast Gothic mansion that now stands up above the Dundee road.

But it is probably the 12th who is best remembered, through the tale that it was only by the courageous ingenuity of his wife that he was prevented from joining Prince Charles Edward in 1746 and so losing all his lands by forfeiture. He had been offended by Cumberland's lack of notice to him when he first paid his respects to the Government side at Dundee and had returned home vowing that he would join the Jacobites. He had reckoned without his wife who had other ideas; under cover of soothing his tired feet in warm water, she poured a kettle of boiling water over them, thus im-mobilising her husband:

> I'm brint, I'm brint, how came it this way?
> I fear I'll no ride for mony a day.
> Send aff the men and to Prince Charlie say:
> 'My heart is with him but I'm tied by the tae'.

> The wily wife flushed, but the laird didna see
> The smile on her face through the tear in her e'e.
> 'Had I kent the guid man wad hae had siccan pain,
> The kettle for me, sud hae coupit its lane.'

The 15th Lord Gray thought on a grand scale and liked his rooms large and ornate; the gallery is 82 feet long and the library 40 ft and the dining and drawing rooms are on the same scale. But he did at least introduce an elementary form of central heating, ahead of his time. And he had 18 gardeners to look after the beautifully laid out gardens.

From the 18th Baroness Gray, the house passed to the Earls of Moray who sold it in 1933 to the Cooperative Holiday Association to be a centre for walkers and others who want to spend their summer holidays in Scotland.

CHAPTER NINE
Perth Today

What then of Perth today? How does it differ from the Perth of 1900? Most notably in size and population. The first sudden increase in numbers had come around 1800 when the city burst its mediaeval bounds but the new building at that time had been on the flat and more easily accessible land. As population continued to grow steadily throughout the century, it became necessary for more and more houses to be sited on the surrounding hills which provide the city's shelter as well as its impressive views. Even on the flat there are few two or three storeyed houses that cannot glimpse from one of their windows some sight of the neighbouring countryside. As the Third Statistical Account records 'during the nineteenth and early twentieth centuries a great many houses of the villa type were built, mostly in the Craigie district and between Cherrybank, formerly an outlying village, and the commercial centre. Before and after the Second World War, privately built houses were extensively sited in the Viewlands and Burghmuir districts in proximity to the new Perth Academy. . . . and since the Second World war, the Corporation has developed large new housing estates in Friarton, Craigie, Letham and Muirton and even one or two high storey blocks'. The author goes on to claim that 'at the time of writing in 1963 Perth's housing record compared favourably with that of any municipality in the country'. If the provision of an adequate number of what a song of the time called 'little boxes' is sufficient, the claim may have been justified, but no one entering the town from the west by the Crieff road just then would have claimed that this development was inspired architecture or even good town planning. Since then, more and more houses have been built in every direction where land is available to house a population that has grown from about 15,000 in 1801 and 29,000 in 1901 to over 40,000 today.

The River Tay frozen at North Inch, Perth, 1895 (*Reproduced by permission of Perth and Kinross District Council Museums and Art Galleries Department, Scotland*).

A second great change (not unrelated to housing and not peculiar to Perth) has been the tremendous improvement in living standards—better and more varied diet, more warmth in the home, more sensible clothing; more jobs open to women and therefore often two separate incomes for the one home; housekeeping has been made less laborious by the use of mechanical devices. Electricity came to Perth at the turn of the century and one has only to think of the large part played in modern life by the vacuum cleaner, the refrigerator and a host of new gadgets. And, with the ever rising standards of living have naturally come ever rising expectations of what constitutes a decent standard of life, especially amongst the young who have never experienced the drudgery endured by their grandmothers. Changing mores have played their part too. As the extended family has almost ceased to exist, both private enterprise and municipal have seen the need for Old Peoples' Homes. At the other end of life, young people have tended to want to leave home sooner and to have their own flat even before they marry or enter into semi-permanent relationships with or without benefit of clergy or registrar, so more and more houses have been converted into flats. And, in Council house districts, more and more new front doors

The City Halls.

appear, the unmistakable sign that the occupier has taken the opportunity of buying his or her own home. Meanwhile the Council has undertaken heroic efforts to refurbish housing which for one reason or another has untimely lapsed into disrepair.

With coming of electricity has come the motor car which has also done much to change the face of every city. Roads have had to be widened wherever possible and resurfaced with asphalt; car parks provided and, in Canal Street, a multi-storey park. With more and more juggernauts on the roads with their noise and smell and shuddering, an attempt has been made to persuade, such vehicles to proceed on their longer journeys *round* instead of *through* Perth by an outer circle Ring Road. Starting just to the south of the town at Craigend, traffic can avoid the built up and busier areas by following a fast dual carriageway, skirting the western edge of the town to a junction with the traffic coming from Glasgow and then that from Crieff until it reaches Dewars roundabout where the town comes to an end and the A9 (vastly improved over the last thirty years) on up to Inverness. Alternatively, the spaghetti junction at Craigend provides a spur to the east which crosses the Tay by the new Friarton bridge. This gives direct access to the A85 to Dundee whence north to Aberdeen, and also to another access lane which can take you along the east bank of the river on to the A93 to Blairgowrie and Braemar or the A94 to Coupar Angus, Forfar and Aberdeen.

The increase in the use of motor traffic of course led to a decrease in the importance of the railways and one branch after another has been closed including that to the west to Crieff and then, under Dr Beeching, the direct and handy line through Glen Farg to the Forth Bridge and Edinburgh, its place being taken by less comfortable buses.

A by-product has been a shift in patterns of employment especially since the closure of the railway workshops. On the whole though there has not been any overwhelming change in industrial pattern. Other industries to lose ground (but not to pass wholly away) have been those of textiles and of dyeing—but the successes of the 19th century in whisky and insurance have continued to grow, even if, in the case of whisky the original businesses have been subject to take-over . . . And the Local Authority has pursued a policy of building advance factories to the south and to the north which have attracted a number of light industries so that Perth has not suffered as much as it might have done from unemployment.

A larger population has meant an increase in trade but it has not been without drawbacks. A great deal has been absorbed by the large supermarkets which are in no way Perth born and bred, even if they do contribute by providing jobs. But one by one the old-fashioned friendly grocers shops have disappeared. And, whereas a dozen years ago, it was possible to write:

> In business, it is not only the giants who make Perth notable. There are an unusually large number of smaller firms which have remained in the day to day control of the same families through several generations and one may be sure of a friendly face and an old-fashioned welcome. Proudfoot's the watchmakers is one, and Hume's the ironmonger; and though Garvie and Syme has moved from the High Street to the southern outskirts it is still run by the Garvies. McEwen's in St John Street is a family firm, and Caird's and Rattray's and Cairncross; Love's has been furnishing for more than a century. . . .

The new shopping mall in the High Street is good of its sort but is a poor exchange for the loss of the family traditions named. None survive under the original ownership, though a somewhat later business, that of Watson's, China merchants, survives as a family run firm.

Yet another breach with the past, to be regretted not only on sentimental grounds, is the loss of the Depot of Perthshire's regiment, the Black Watch. Their barracks were built originally for cavalry in the 1790s and first used by the Black Watch in 1830. From 1882 they were the HQ of the 42nd Regimental District until 1904 when the name was changed to the Depot until 1961. The subsequent demolition of the old buildings radically changed the area behind the Epis-copalian Cathedral where once stood the wood of Drumhar but the elaborate Royal Coat of Arms was carefully dismantled and re-erected at the new Queen's Barracks in the Dunkeld Road (see page).

With the rise in living standards has come a great improvement in health and in life expectancy which has increased by twenty years or so in the 20th century. Old killers such as typhoid and tuberculosis have been virtually extinguished with improved medical knowledge, enabling hospitals opened specially to deal with them, to be closed, and resources concentrated in a few larger General Hospitals.

Perth has been exceptionally fortunate in this respect. Its out-of-date old infirmary in York Place, dating from 1838, was transferred to new and better equipped buildings, declared open by King George V in 1914 and these have been steadily updated since. It was one of the first hospitals in Scotland to exploit the use of X Rays.

In addition, the citizens have had access to the hutted hospital built at Bridge of Earn for emergencies at the start of the 1939–45 War. Ugly outside, its doctors surgeons and nurses gained a high reputation for the work that they were able to do inside, which latterly concentrated more and more on orthopaedic cases. 50 years old its temporary accommodation has served its purpose and its work is, at the present time, being transferred to the Perth Royal Infirmary as that complex is steadily extended up the hill westwards.

The site of the former hospital in York Place was cleared in 1992 to make way for a multi-million pound Public Library and District Library Headquarters. The shell of the Old Infirmary building has been retained as a building of architectural interest; it will be used as the formal entrance to the Library with an exhibition area and cafeteria on the ground floor and administration offices and meeting rooms above.

New building to blend with the old, comprising 400 square metres, will house the District Library Headquarters and mobile libraries, lending libraries for adults and children, reference and local studies libraries, archives and a small theatre.

Now Perth has taken another step forward with the completion of new buildings costing well over twenty million pounds to bring the Perth Royal Infirmary once more up to date and to increase its capacity by almost double to an estimated 453 beds plus 25 day spaces and 25 day beds. The older wards are being transformed for other purposes and patients will be nursed in the new wards with the most up to date facilities. There will be five new theatres in addition to the two new ones already in use in the new maternity wing, an improved out-patient department and new accident provision. Amongst other new or extended facilities will be those for occupational therapy, speech therapy, and hydrotherapy, and modern equipment for radiology, both diagnostic and therapeutic. The new buildings were opened by H.R.H. The Princess Royal on August 25th 1993. Meanwhile the enlarged Murray Royal continues its good work.

Equally important are the dental and other medical services which now visit the schools to forestall possible later troubles and the ever faithful district nurses who, with the aid of Home Helps, enable many ill and old folks to remain (to their great happiness) in their own homes—as do the Marie Curie nurses and the MacMillan foundation to care for cancer patients.

Perth is also fortunate in its old peoples' residential homes, some of which have already been mentioned and its sheltered housing. Amongst them, and worthy of special mention, is Bowerswell House. After the Second World War, the City's official Memorial to its dead was to convert it into a Home for the elderly, which was opened by Princess Margaret in 1950; forty years later the house itself has been renovated and £1.5 million has been spent by The Forteviot Charitable Trust, Scottish Homes and Perth and Kinross District Council to make it the centre of an extended sheltered housing project which Princess Margaret returned to inaugurate in May 1992.

With the growth in population and the raising of the school leaving age the old Academy could no longer meet the demands for schooling and was moved to a magnificent site up at Viewlands in the 1920s but even their enlarged and more modern buildings did not suffice for long. A new secondary school was built in North Muirton, unfortunately at a time when construction materials were hard to come by. It has revived the name of the Grammar School and stands next to St Columba's, the Roman Catholic secondary school.

Last to come is the High School, product of the 60s, also up at Viewlands. All are not only modernly equipped within, but surrounded by their own playing fields.

As for provision for continuing education, Perth lost out to a suggestion that it was the ideal situation for Scotland's newest university to Stirling but it has its College of Further Education, founded in 1961 and, since 1971, located on high ground alongside the Crieff Road, where it claims to be the largest Centre of Open Learning in the country. It offers the widest academic courses, and with a motto of 'Making it happen'. It offers training in:

> Marketing, Sales, Personnel, Accounting, European Law, Languages, Time management, Training Needs Analysis, Information Technology, CAD/CAM, Construction Technology, Hotel Management, and Tourism to name but a few. . . .
> 'Be ahead of the Field
> Let Perth College make it for you'.

Perhaps Perth may yet have its university.

Another sphere in which greater expectations (and greater philanthropy on the part of those who had already done much) was that of increased and more sophisticated sporting facilities. Those of the Bell's Indoor Sports Centre (since renamed the Gannochy Trust Sports Centre) have already been mentioned; opened in the Sixties and enlarged several times since. A vast new Pleasure Pool to replace our old-fashioned if much loved swimming Pool in the Dunkeld Road has arisen on the Glasgow Road where a new Dewar's Ice rink has also been constructed; new courts for the Perth Tennis Club in Hay Street; new Squash Courts there and across the river at Bridgend;—the shift has been ever outward, leaving the Dunkeld Road mainly a line of garages with one enormous supermarket where the former Muirton Park football ground once stood. Indeed it was the purchase of this site that facilitated the most spectacular of all the advances—a new home for the St Johnstone Football Club.

The change here could not have come at a more opportune moment. St Johnstone had not prospered since the days of Willie Ormond and Henry Hall in 1971. Membership of the Premier League in 1975 was short lived, as it was again in 1982, and, by 1986 we had slipped through the First Division to half way down the Second, with support for the Club ever dwindling. A new Chairman in Geoff Brown and a new manager in Alex Totten and a large injection of cash was beginning to turn the tide but the old ground could never have met new safety regulations called for after the Hillsborough disaster. The Club had one valuable asset; it was sitting on a very valuable site which Asda wanted. But every sort of complication followed, only for one difficulty after another to be surmounted by the new Board; and even then there was the problem of a new site. Gordon Bannerman's recently published history of the last few years of the Club's history may take up the story. 'The 17-acre package of land required out on the Crieff Road at Newton of Huntingtower secured through the generosity of Perthshire farmer Bruce McDiarmid was a crucial element in the tortuous wheeling and dealing which had consumed so much of the board's attention month after month.

Initial links were forged between club and land owner through Bob Reid, a local quantity surveyor and nephew of Bruce McDiarmid. St Johnstone owned Muirton Park and the

McDiarmid Park football ground.

adjacent Florence Place car park and they had taken some time to clear the path to the new stadium with feu superior, Lord Mansfield, whose family had gifted the Dunkeld Road land. Any new stadium, however, would have remained little more than a pipe dream but for the McDiarmid connection. In an intricate and, at times, an exasperating jigsaw this was the telling piece.

'The going rate for the land would have been around £400,000 and, quite simply, St Johnstone simply couldn't look at that kind of money. We couldn't even raise a quarter of that sum. But we hoped Bruce McDiarmid might be interested in helping out the club and the city of Perth' said Brown.

'The land was made available to Saints because Bruce saw the club as being an important part of Perth life. He saw this as a gift to the people of the city and I would like to think Bruce saw how hard people had worked voluntarily in the interests of the football club.'

The berry and barley fields were transformed as the bachelor farmer, in his late seventies, accepted a 20 per cent shareholding in St Johnstone and, at the board's insistence, the honorary presidency of the football club.'

And so St Johnstone got the first all-seater stadium in the country swiftly followed by promotion to the Premier League again, even if given little chance by the pundits of remaining there. Halfway through the season they were standing fourth in the table, with Europe within their sights. Even at the end of the season, their placing was seventh and the club was financially on a sounder footing than at any previous time in its history. Another good season followed but it remains to be seen how the Club will fare after dispensing with the services of Alex Totten.

All this might sound as though Perth was a city only for young athletes but such has never been the case. The early years of the present century were those which provided a home for Perth' most distinguished poet, William Soutar who sadly died (in 1943) too young after a long debilitating illness. He was equally at home writing in English (as in his poignant 'No man outlives the grief of war') and in Scots; in humour as well as sadness as in 'Ae Nicht at Amulree' . . . His likeness stands as a memorial in the museum.

In recent years, in recognition of Soutar's achievement as one of the best Scots poets, the District Library Service has established the William Soutar Writer's Fellowship. A writer in residence is appointed each year to encourage interest in literature and Scots poetry in particular. The residency is based at Soutar's former home in Wilson Street, Perth which is used as a centre for literary groups.

Associated with this development a Scots Language Resource Centre has been established in the Perth Library to

Posthumous bust of William Soutar, by Benno Schotz, 1959. Bronze (*Reproduced by permission of Perth and Kinross District Council Museums and Art Galleries Department, Scotland*).

preserve and foster Scots Language. The Resource Centre staff have ambitious plans including a nationwide survey of regional Scot's usage and a data base of Scots in published literature.

Perth also has its Society to encourage creative writing and its painters have an annual Show in the Art Gallery attached to the Museum. It has its Symphony Orchestra and its Choral Society which give concerts in the City Hall; a Dramatic Society and an Operatic Society, and a highly successful Youth Orchestra which has travelled and performed abroad.

The possession of a thriving repertory theatre is one of the attractions of Perth which has long had a tradition of dramatic entertainment, going back to the mediaeval plays of the Crafts and of the boys of the Grammar School—through special performances laid on for distinguished visitors—to the 18th century playhouses. The first of these stood in South Street opposite the entrance to Princes Street and was housed in the building vacated when the Grammar School moved to combine with the Perth Academy in its new building in Rose Terrace. Mr and Mrs Siddons played here for a time but the theatre did not have a long life for, like Drury Lane and many others, it went up in flames. Then, for the first half of the 19th century, there was a theatre on the corner of Atholl Street and Kinnoull Street. The present Perth Theatre in the High Street was built at the start of this century; it has had its ups and downs but has enjoyed a remarkable success during the last fourteen years under the management of Miss Joan Knight. It was recently completely refurbished, backstage and front, and reopened in the presence of H.R.H. Princess Alexandra. Not only are its regular programmes well attended but there is an annual pantomime which is a delight to thousands of local children.

Professionally the highlight for the Arts is the annual Festival in May when musicians of distinction provide a fortnight of music and the arts generally. It has even been visited by Scottish Ballet which danced in the Theatre and included a much appreciated matinee at half price for senior citizens. One such, I remember, coincided with the hottest afternoon of the year but no casualties were reported from either side of the footlights.

The Museum is a 'must' for visitors and citizens alike and for both old and young. Specially to be visited are its recently rearranged Natural History Gallery and its new display illustrating the history of the town and its occupations.

Another comparatively new adornment to the town has been the way in which the Council have beautified its streets and, in partnership with local sponsorship have made them bloom, while for those interested in gardens, there has been since 1968 the National Trust's Branklyn Garden.

Another garden of a totally different kind has been created at Cherrybank around the H.Q. of Bell's whisky. It is devoted not only to the widest range of heathers (600 varieties in 60,000 plants to say nothing of another 45,000 shrubs) but as a place for families to visit, it also has a tea room and an amusement area for children. This may be reached by the Glasgow road which also houses at number 107, the Youth Hostel.

At the other end of the scale, Perth today would not be itself if it did not have one picturesque but complete anomaly, its company of High Constables, an institution shared only by Holyrood, Edinburgh and the Port of Leith. They were in existence before 1466 as a sort of police force to enable the magistrates to enforce law and order, but they have not been called out in that capacity since 1843 when some soldiers ran amok. Now, as in the case of the Queen's Body-guard for Scotland, their's is a dignified rather than a martial role.

1967 was an important year for the well being of Perth since it saw the foundation of its Civic Trust to 'bring together all those concerned about Perth's fine buildings, amenities, and the quality of proposed developments, and to keep a watch on buildings of architectural or historic interest and any proposed alterations to them;' it examines planning ap-plications and sends an observer to relevant council meetings; it promotes Civic Trust Awards for restored and new buildings of merit; publishes information about Perth to help people appreciate their heritage, and organises lectures, meetings and guided walks around the historical parts of Perth.

One of the inspirers and a driving force was the late Mrs Margaret Stewart PhD. She had formed the archaeological Section of the long-lived Perth Society of Natural Science but that did not reach a wide enough constituency for the above purposes. She was the first Chairman of the Civic Trust; she edited and contributed to *Perth. A Town Survey* which consisted of a series of articles by members of the Trust which had been published at intervals in the Perthshire Advertiser'. Four years later she published a survey of the city with the impassioned title *It will soon be too late*. When excavations were undertaken by the Scottish Urban Archaeological Trust, she formed and was Chairman of a support group and earned from the excavators a well-deserved tribute for her 'energy, commitment and enthusiasm . . . an inspiration to us all'. She had also, much earlier, contributed to the Council's own booklet of encouragement, entitled 'Walks in Perth' 1972.

Another pioneer in making the buildings of Perth more widely known to its citizens has been Miss R. Fothergill who stimulated her pupils in the Caledonian Road and the Kinnoull primary schools to find out and record what they could learn from street names and similar sources about their locality, resulting in pamphlets on 'Kinnoull, Bridgend and Barnhill' and 'What's in a Name'. More recently, the public as well as the Trust has benefited by a *Short History of Perth* researched and written by the historian Marion L. Stavert now in its second edition. Others have contributed by pamphlets on special aspects which can be bought from Perth & Kinross District Libraries.

Another organisation with the welfare of Perth in view has recently been formed, less perhaps with its past in mind than its future, though the preservation of what is memorable is also one of its stated aims—The Perth Partnership. Its partners include The Scottish Development Agency, Perth and Kinross District Council and Tayside Regional Council together with private enterprise which is strongly represented on its committee. Its Chairman is the Corporate Affairs Director of United Distillers U.K.; General Accident is represented too and, of smaller enterprises, McEwens of Perth. The Chairman's first Annual Report for 1990 sets out its aims. 'Visually' he writes 'the town has never looked better. The new pedestrianisation (of the High Street) and signposting schemes have created a most attractive environment which has been further advanced by the vigorous Pride in Perth and Perth in Bloom campaigns which we have supported. Business confidence has been boosted via the opening of the Shore Road business complex and the Retail Park. In this first year, Perth Partnership has helped to lay foundations for the future growth of Perth. In partnership we have been successful in raising not only local confidence but also creating a better business awareness of Perth and its potential . . . I believe that the Perth Partnership has shown that the Private and Public sectors can work well together and this will form a model for future development especially once Scottish Enterprise is with us next year.' Other aims are to encourage tourism and the use of the city as a Conference Centre using a 450 seater auditorium and, hopefully a Four Star Hotel. Already achieved has been the tidying up of two central sites which were unworthy of their location whatever useful purposes they served—the Skinnergate and the Mill Street bus and taxi stances, and the open access to the lade behind Marks & Spencer.

The Partnership also looks forward to working with the Civic Trust itself and the Scottish Urban Archaeological Trust which has its HQ in Perth, and has done so much to throw light on its past.

CHAPTER TEN

Exploring from Perth

The neighbourhood of Perth is rich in places to visit, whether for natural beauty or for historical or architectural interest and a few suggestions may be helpful for those planning expeditions within a range of about 40 miles.

The countryside is thick with castles, large and small, ruined and restored, some occupied and therefore likely to be open to the public only in connection with the Scottish Gardens scheme, others unoccupied and under public control. To the north, Glamis, though still a home, is open throughout the summer and is outstanding in every way and has something to offer to all the family. Ardblair near Blairgowrie is of special interest to Jacobites because of the number of relics of Prince Charlie brought from Gask by the Oliphants after intermarriage with the Blairs. They include the Prince's Garter, of a paler blue than that worn by the Hanoverians; his gloves and spurs; some rough, thin leather shoes he wore when he was passing as Betty Burke; his crucifix and a number of his letters, including a long one to his father, telling him of his success at Prestonpans, but saying that he could take little pleasure in a victory over men who were his fellow-countrymen. The house is also a museum of Oliphant family history, with portraits of all the lairds from the 17th century onwards, and of the second Lord Nairne whose daughter married an Oliphant—and a whole room is furnished with the possessions of Carolina Oliphant, the poetess Lady Nairne, who began and ended her days at Gask; only towards the end of her life did she admit authorship of works which included not only Jacobite songs such as 'Will ye no' come back again' and family pieces such as 'The Auld Hoose', but also 'Caller Herring' and 'the Laird of Cockpen'. This, too, is a family house very much lived in, although open to the public by special arrangement through the local tourist office.

Further to the north-west is the Duke of Atholl's Blair Castle with 13th, 16th, and 18th century additions. In the first room, there are portraits of James V and his queen, and of Mary Queen of Scots and her son James VI. The civil war royalists are in the next room where there is contemporary furniture, a portrait of Montrose, the helmet and breastplate of Claverhouse and one of the original copies of the Covenant of 1638. The later Jacobite Murrays have their memorial upstairs with a bed covered with tartan material 200 years old, said to have been formerly on a circular bed in which slept all the seventeen sons of Sir David Murray of Tullibardine. Few houses can have such a wealth of pictures and furnishings all set off in rooms with splendid fireplaces and plaster ceilings, spacious and well-lit by the large 18th century windows. And the interest is much enhanced by the photostats everywhere of the bills for the original purchases of the items.

Their collections can only be rivalled by those at the Palace of Scone, also lived in but open to the public from April to October. Priceless porcelain, pictures, ivories and furniture. Also parkland with Highland cattle and Jacob's sheep, woodland garden and pinetum. Here, on the Moot Hill, the Scottish Kings were enthroned on the Stone of Destiny.

Smaller castles, partly ruined but well worth a visit include Elcho, just to the east of Perth (take the road signposted to Rhynd just before you join the motorway to Edinburgh); and there are several in and around Dundee especially Broughty Castle and Claypotts, one of the best, unaltered, Z-plan Tower Houses surviving (Most of the castles astride the Perth to Dundee road are still private homes but some are open from time to time under the Gardens scheme).

To the south is Balvaird Castle on A912 off Glenfarg; Burleigh Castle, just east of Milnathort (admission on application to the key-holder at the farm opposite), and Loch Leven Castle, on which Mary Queen of Scots was imprisoned and from which she escaped. It is situated on an island but can be reached by a ferry which runs from the shore beneath the wall of Kinross House.

Scone Palace. (*Photo by Perthshire Tourist Board*).

In Fife, there are Aberdour Castle, well-cared for by the Scottish Development Department with extensive remains from 13th to 17th centuries, set in gardens; Kellie Castle, now given to the National Trust for Scotland, also in a lovely garden—two 14th century towers joined by a 16th century range; and Falkland Palace. Most of what we can see here was built by James IV and embellished by James V. Both loved the place and the hunting and hawking which it provided, as did Mary Queen of Scots and the last King to occupy it, James VI. The most splendid part is the south range, essentially Renaissance both in conception and detail. Its buttress columns and its medallions are similar to French work of the same date and it has been called the best of tributes to the Auld Alliance. Inside is a Royal Chapel which retains more of the original decoration than any other part of the building; the carved wooden screen at the entrance is original, with its hand-turned pillars, each different. The east range is roofless but scarcely less impressive and here has been recreated a bedchamber such as James's V's would have been with crowns, monograms and coats of arms in brilliant heraldic colours—and a four-poster bed with gold hangings as the centre piece. In the garden there is a long stretch of lawn, flanked with with beds of iris and lupin and climbing roses, ceonothus, viburnum and weigelia. And, at the end, is a royal tennis court which can still be played in and is only rivalled for age by that at Hampton Court.

To the west of Perth are Huntingtower and Methven Castle, recently restored by the present resident owners but open from time to time for concerts in aid of charity. Drummond Castle has magnificent Italianate formal gardens, regularly open on certain days during the summer and a 1490 tower house beside its Victorian mansion.

Just over thirty miles from Perth is Stirling Castle with site and buildings every bit as exciting as those of Edinburgh with its Great Hall, Renaissance Palace, chapel and museum of the Argyll and Sutherland Highlanders. Argyll's Lodging is worth a visit and, nearby, Wallace Memorial Tower and Bannockburn. Another ten miles brings you to Doune one of the largest ruined castles in the whole of Scotland.

Scotland has never been able to equal South Britain in the size or the number of its medieval ecclesiastical remains but it is surprising how many of its gems are within forty miles of Perth.

In Dunfermline, the abbey dominates all. Beneath the church that we see today—the work of Queen Margaret's son, David I, that 'sair saint for the crown'—are the foundations of two earlier buildings, a small Culdee church and that of Malcolm Canmore of around 1074 in which he and Margaret are buried. She had been married at Dunfermline, her children were born there, and though she died in Edinburgh, she was brought back to rest there, as were six later Scottish kings. The great Norman nave was modelled on Durham, and its massive pillars and severe round arches give the impression of strength rather than beauty. But there *is* beauty to be found once one's eyes have attuned themselves to the dim light, especially in the arcading round the walls. On the floor the out-lines of the earlier churches are indicated by a brass strip, and five gridded openings which can be illuminated to show traces of the earlier masonry. In place of the original eastern end of the church which had fallen into decay, a dignified Gothic building in the Perpendicular style was put up in the 19th century to serve as the parish kirk. At the junction between the old and the new stands the tomb of Robert the Bruce. As interesting and even more impressive are the ruins of the Benedictine monastery, built in the 13th century, burnt by Edward I in 1303, and rebuilt in the 14th century.

The cathedral of Dunkeld likewise combines a magnificent ruin with an active Presbyterian kirk, but in this case it is the choir that has survived—with some restoration. Ironically its finest treasure is the tomb of the sacrilegious destroyer of Elgin Cathedral, the wolf of Badenoch, son of Robert II. The nave dates from the 15th century; though roofless, it has peace and an undeniable grandeur, with its massive pillars supporting pointed arches with triforium and clerestory above. Its destruction was not intended—was, indeed, contrary to Argyll's detailed instructions.

Dunkeld has a fine site overlooking the River Tay but Dunblane Cathedral runs it close with the Allan Water. Its oldest part is its tower because it belongs to an older church than the one we see today. Norman in style, four storeys of it were built in about 1100 and two added later—the whole surmounted by a parapet of 1500 and a small but effective spire. Next comes the Lady Chapel, and then the choir from the 13th century and the nave a hundred years later. The east window is glorious—narrow pointed lancets crowned with an unusual rose made up of three trefoils—and so is some of the woodwork especially the miserere seats on either side of the communion table, and the Chisholm stalls at the west end, deeply carved and among the earliest examples of their kind in Scotland. From the outside the west door is exceptionally elaborate. And above the west window there is the vesica of which Ruskin wrote 'I know not anything so perfect in its simplicity, and so beautiful, as far as it reaches, in all the Gothic with which I am acquainted'.

The chief glory of Brechin is not the largely rebuilt cathedral but the much older round tower built by the Culdee community which flourished there before ever a bishop came. The tower, the only one of its sort in Scotland other than that of Abernethy dates from about 1000 A.D. and follows the Irish pattern, notably in the case of its doorway, with figures of the crucifixion above the arch, and clerics on either side, one with the conventional curved pastoral staff, the other with the much older T-shaped cross. Apart from the raising of the earth level round about, and the loss of its internal wooden floors, the tower of red sandstone blocks still stands as it was built except for the spire which was added in the 14th century.

Little now remains of the great cathedral church of St Andrews but there is so much else; its university, its castle, its beautiful St Salvators Collegiate church, its little chapel of St Leonard and the large Town Kirk dedicated in 1410 to the Holy Trinity; its ancient West Port and, of course, its Links. For all that, time must be left to explore the precincts of the Cathedral and its museum.

The other abbeys of which extensive remains survive lie to the north—Restenneth in remote and beautiful countryside and Arbroath. Restenneth was founded by Nechtan, King of the Picts when he adopted Christianity and has possibly the oldest fragment of church architecture in Scotland. Arbroath dates from 1178 when William The Lion dedicated his abbey to St Thomas a' Canterbury. Warm red stone was used and it is a lovely place in the sunshine. Not the least impressive feature is the sumptuous dwelling for the Abbot, now finely restored after many years of neglect and misuse during which it first was used a factory and then as a private house. Its contents include a beautiful fifteenth century (headless) effigy of a saint, probably Becket, and a quaint headstone carving of Death catching up with old age.

Richest in interesting smaller churches is the coastline of Fife—the golden fringe as James VI called it. This is a 'must' anyway to see the fishing towns from Culross all the way to Crail. The abbey church at Culross has a Romanesque doorway, a 17th century wooden pulpit and, in the Bruce aisle, an ornate tomb of Sir George Bruce with his wife and eight children. A few miles on, is the unusual square church of Burntisland, said to have been the first church built specifically for Presbyterian worship. Others worth visiting are Upper Largo, St Monans and Crail while a little way inland is another church, Dairsie unusual because it dates from the temporary revival of Episcopacy 1621. Leuchars has one of the few remaining Romanesque churches.

North of the Tay, Dundee has an appropriately large burgh church and Fowlis Easter has a 15th century painting of the crucifixion and other treasures with the result that it has to be kept locked but the key can be obtained by enquiring in the village. It must not be confused with Fowlis Wester on the other side of Perth and almost into Crieff. This has a Pictish stone within and a remarkable Pictish Cross on the village green.

Another church which is worth hunting out by the enthusiast is Grandtully (sign-posted but not easy to find—persist up the track, which is feasible for cars, through the first farm, and, a few hundred yards beyond, stop at the second farm); behind it is the church, looking like a long low barn from the outside. He may also wish to seek out the two Collegiate churches of Tullibardine and Innerpeffray. In the latter case, there is the added bonus of the oldest free library in Scotland, founded in the 17th century and placed in its present building in 1750. Finally, if you find yourself at Weem, visit the church for the sake of its 17th century monument to Sir Alexander Menzies's wives, mother, grandmother, great grandmother and great-great-grandmother.

Other places which may be of interest include Folk museums at Glamis and at Ceres; a clan museum for the Robertsons at Bruar (north of Blair Atholl; a fisheries museum at Anstruther and of motors at Doune. Dundee has a well-arranged museum on a scale fitting the city's size and importance and, in its docks, the restored HMS *Unicorn* with Captain Scott's *Discovery* to keep it company. The whole village of Culross is a museum in itself as is that of Falkland, thanks to the National Trust for Scotland. Distilleries may be toured at Blair

Atholl and at Pitlochry which also has a renowned theatre and a fish ladder at which salmon can be seen making their way up the river to spawn—as they also can be seen, in the autumn, frantically trying to leap up the falls at Buchanty Spout in Glenalmond. There is a safari park at Blair Drummond; sailing and water-skiing on Loch Earn; mountains to ascend such as Schiehallion and Ben Lawers, the latter unequalled in Britain for its Alpine flora. Golf courses surround Perth, with those at St Andrews, Gleneagles and Blairgowrie on the outer circle. For bird lovers there is an observation post at Vane Farm on Loch Leven and a bird sanctuary by the Loch of Lowes from which ospreys may be seen. Birnam Woods and Dunsinane may be visited provided one remembers that Macbeth was in fact killed far to the north at Lumphanan in Aberdeenshire, and anyway had more to be said for him than Duncan. And no-one should miss seeing the beech hedge alongside the road at Meikleour, first planted in 1846 and now over 100 feet high and trimmed every six years.

Anyone interested in gardens should invest in the pamphlet published annually of those open to the public from time to time, because these are bound to vary from year to year; but special mention may be made of Edzell because of its 16th century lay out and of Drummond Castle designed in the Italian manner and of Falkland, Kinross, Glamis, and Scone open most days throughout the summer.

Finally, the district is rich in Pictish crosses and other carvings such as those in the Perth Museum, and in the collections housed in the museums at St Vigean's and Meigle, and, in the open, at Glamis and by the roadside at Aberlemno. And there are souterrains at Carlungie and Ardestie which can be seen, just to the north of Dundee. For a layman's introduction see the present author's *Portrait of Perth, Angus and Fife*, pages 14–17, available in the Local History Room of the Sandeman Library. Better still would be to buy the scholarly and more recent *The Picts* by Anna Ritchie (1989).

If by this time the visitor is not exhausted, he or she can address themselves to the unsolved problem of the Picts and the mysterious signs or symbols on the many stones which they erected on the lands which they once dominated to the north-east of Perth. On the earliest stones the symbols are incised while the later ones are beautifully carved in relief, using only the simplest of tools, and the symbols gradually give way to Christian motifs. Two small museums at Meigle and St Vigeans provide a easy introduction as do those in the churchyard at Eassie and near Aberlemno. For an academic background, the reader is recommended to works by I. Henderson (published by Thames and Hudson) and by Anna Ritchie (HMSO), both of which can normally be consulted in the Sandeman Library.

Index